LAURA INGALLS WILDER
A Biography

LAURA INGALLS WILDER

A Biography

by William Anderson

HarperCollins*Publishers*

Laura Ingalls Wilder
A Biography

For information address HarperCollins Children's Books,
a division of HarperCollins Publishers,
10 East 53rd Street, New York, NY 10022.
Typography by Al Cetta
1   2   3   4   5   6   7   8   9   10
First Edition

❖

Library of Congress Cataloging-in-Publication Data
Anderson, William, date
  Laura Ingalls Wilder : a biography / by William Anderson.
      p.   cm.
  Includes index.
  Summary: A biography of the writer whose pioneer life on the American
prairie became the basis for her "Little House" books.
  ISBN 0-06-020113-4. — ISBN 0-06-020114-2 (lib. bdg.)
  1. Wilder, Laura Ingalls, 1867-1957—Biography—Juvenile literature.
2. Authors, American—20th century—Biography—Juvenile literature.
3. Frontier and pioneer life—United States—Juvenile literature.
4. Children's stories—Authorship—Juvenile literature.   [1. Wilder, Laura
Ingalls, 1867-1957.   2. Authors, American.   3. Frontier and pioneer life.]
I. Title.
PS3545.I342Z555   1992   91-33805
813'.52—dc20   CIP
[B]   AC

Contents

Acknowledgments

The writing of this biography of Laura Ingalls Wilder has been, in many ways, similar to the creation of the "Little House" books themselves. The people and places and events described here are the results of reliance on detailed memories, written historical accounts, and the lively essence of Laura's eventful life.

For the facts, I used the resources of the Herbert Hoover Presidential Library in West Branch, Iowa; the Laura Ingalls Wilder Home Association in Mansfield, Missouri; and the Laura Ingalls Wilder Memorial Society in De Smet, South Dakota. These sources supplied the historical background for this book.

For the flashes of Laura's character that I hope are found in this biography, I am grateful to the many people who witnessed her life and shared their firsthand memories with me. They, or their families, know who they are, and I am confident that the book is enriched by their generous sharing of oral history.

The help and cooperation of Vivian Glover of the Laura Ingalls Wilder Memorial Society in De Smet helped clarify many facts of the prairie life described in this biography. Connie Tidwell of the Laura Ingalls Wilder Home Association in Mansfield checked details and provided her own impressions regarding the Wilders' lives on Rocky Ridge Farm.

Virginia Ann Koeth, who edited this book at Harper Children's Books, helped me many times to say what I had to say in a clear and accurate fashion.

W. T. A.

Foreword

During the Civil War, the American government passed a law that had no connection with the fighting that was separating the North and the South. When President Abraham Lincoln signed his name to a document creating the Homestead Act of 1862, an exciting opportunity became available to all Americans. It was the chance to claim—for free—open lands belonging to the United States government, especially in the areas that made up the American West.

Beyond the Mississippi River, all the way to the Pacific coastline, lay millions of acres of land. Some parts of this area were called the Great American Desert and were thought to be too dry and unfit for farming. However, much of the land west of the Mississippi was prairie country, covered by miles of waving grasses. Few trees grew there, but the soil was fertile and black and open for settlement.

Each American citizen over the age of twenty-one was eligible to file a claim for the government homestead land. The open plains had been surveyed and divided into squares of 160 acres (one quarter of a square mile) each. On maps the plotted land looked like a mammoth checkerboard. In the 1860's, most of the land was unoccupied, waiting for settlers to arrive.

There were only a few requirements for filing land claims. The homesteader had to register his claim officially at a land office, where records were kept. A house had to be built on the claim and the prairie plowed up to show that in the future a farm would exist. For six months each year, the homesteader or a family member must live on the property. Some homesteaders hired "claim sitters" to fulfill this requirement. They were people paid to live on the land and protect it from being taken over by claim jumpers.

At the end of five years, when all the government specifications were met, the land became the homesteader's property. The government issued a "patent," a deedlike document that meant that the homestead ownership passed from the United

States federal government to the man or woman who had developed it as a farm and home.

The Homestead Act was exciting news for many Americans. Where else would a government give a citizen land just for the asking? A happy song was sung, describing the Homestead Act:

Oh come to this country
and have no fear of harm,
Our Uncle Sam is rich enough
To give us all a farm!

In America's eastern towns, villages and crowded farming neighborhoods, people were lured by the stories of good hunting, level, rich farmlands and the chance to pioneer in the American West. People were proud to be Americans, able to live in a country so wide and rich and free.

When the Civil War ended in 1865, thousands of soldiers and civilians decided to head west to see what lay beyond the great river, the Mississippi. The river represented a dividing line between East and West. "The Great River Road," as it was called, split America from north to south. It flowed from its headwaters in Minnesota to the port of New Orleans in the South, where it emptied into the Gulf of Mexico. The Mississippi was not only a north-south waterway; it was also a crossroads for pioneers traveling west in the direction of the sunsets.

Just five years after the Homestead Act became part of American history, a baby girl was born deep in the forest only seven miles from the Mississippi. Her entire life was shaped by the westward movement. She was Laura Ingalls Wilder. She first lived the life of a pioneer girl and then, when the experience of the frontier was memory, wrote down her tales of growing up in the West. Her stories, known as the "Little House" books, have given the world a sharp, clear picture of life in the woods and on the plains during the last phase of American pioneering, from the 1860's to the 1890's. But when Laura Elizabeth Ingalls was born in 1867, in a log cabin near Pepin, Wisconsin, no one imagined the remarkable person she would become, first as a pioneer and then as a much-loved author.

The importance of Laura's work as the author of the "Little House" books is that she recorded a period of American life that historians call westward expansion. During her experiences as a pioneer girl and then as a farmer's wife, Laura Ingalls Wilder was too busy living her life to write about it. Only after she was sixty did she think about writing of the pioneering people and adventures she remembered so well.

Laura explained that her desire to write came from her feeling that what she had experienced on the prairies were "stories that had to be told." She said that her memories of pioneer days "were altogether too good to be lost."

"I wanted the children now to understand more about the beginnings of things," Laura said, "to know what is behind the things they see—what it is that made America as they know it. Then I thought of writing the story of my childhood in several volumes—an eight-volume historical novel covering every aspect of the American frontier."*

Laura's plan to write about the frontier was a project that would have kept any other historian researching and writing for years. But the history she wove into the "Little House" stories was close and familiar to her. Because she had lived it, Laura could describe life as a pioneer in a way history books could not. "I understood that in my own life I rep-

---

*Fourteen years after her death a ninth manuscript of Laura's was published: *The First Four Years* (Harper & Row, 1971).

resented a period of American history," she marveled.

As a writer, Laura possessed what few authors do: enough personal adventures and information to write without extensive research. "I had seen the whole frontier," Laura wrote, "the woods, the Indian country of the great plains, the frontier towns, the building of railroads in wild, unsettled country, homesteading and farms coming in to take possession. I realized that I had seen and lived it all—all the successive phases of the frontier, first the frontiersman, then the pioneer, then the farmers, and the towns."

Through Laura's keen memories, her sharp vision and her storytelling skill, we can still experience the pioneer West as she saw it.

In the "Little House" books, Laura Ingalls Wilder recorded her life and the lives of her own family and friends as they created homes in the wilderness. The memories Laura shared were of lives well lived, filled with courage and kindness, adventure and accomplishment.

1. A Pioneer Family

When Laura Ingalls was born in the woods in the state of Wisconsin, the land there was still raw and wild. The region was called "The Big Woods" because the forests stretched out for miles toward the bluffs of the Mississippi River to the west and on to Lake Superior to the north. Panthers and bears and deer roamed through the brush, and the big trees grew thick enough to blot out the sky overhead. Only the coming of a few trappers, hunters and farmers made the countryside seem slightly civilized. Still, miles often separated one frontier farm from the next.

Laura's parents, Charles and Caroline Ingalls, were Wisconsin pioneers. Her father, Charles Philip Ingalls, was born near Cuba, New York, in 1836. His boyhood was spent with a big family of eight brothers and sisters moving west with their parents, Lansford and Laura Ingalls. When Charles was nine, the family lived in the state of Illinois, just west of a growing frontier town called Chicago. Then they traveled north into Wisconsin, settling close to the Oconomowoc River, near the village of Concord.

Working with his father and his brothers on their family farm, Charles grew strong and straight and keen in the ways of the woods. He learned to be a shrewd frontiersman, meeting new difficulties and hardships with spirit and skill. Making the new land produce enough food for the Ingalls family was a challenge that Charles, his brothers and their father conquered together. When work was slack on their own place, the Ingalls boys worked for other farmers. They brought home the money they earned, to help buy shoes and schoolbooks for the younger brothers and sisters. Peter and Charles were the oldest; then came Lydia, Polly, Lansford James, Laura Ladocia, Hiram, George and Ruby.

For Charles Ingalls, attending the neighborhood schools was possible only when he could be spared from farm work. But he quickly realized the importance of reading and writing and all knowledge. He learned to write his name, Charles P. Ingalls, with a flourish, and he became a good speller. His family were all good storytellers, but Charles also liked to read. When he was seventeen, a hard-earned $1.25 left his pocket to buy a scroll-covered two-volume set of books called *The Life of Napoleon*.

Growing up in the Wisconsin woods along the Oconomowoc River, Charles not only learned to be a skilled carpenter, trapper, woodsman, hunter and farmer. He also learned to sing and dance and play songs and hymns on a honey-colored fiddle. No one in the family remembered how Charles Ingalls first acquired a violin; perhaps he bought it from a traveling peddler or traded for it with a neighbor. By the time he was a teenager, Charles and his fiddle had started a lifetime of making music together.

The Ingalls family sat around the fireplace through long winter evenings listening to the music Charles fiddled, and soon the neighbors knew where they could find rollicking, foot-tapping tunes. Charles Ingalls was so jolly and so bold a fiddler he was a popular addition to the neighborhood frolics. The Ingalls children attended spelling schools, hot-maple-sugar parties, sleigh rides and corn-husking socials. But the dances were the most exciting events of all.

Ingalls and Wilder homesites and places of interest

At harvest parties or wedding dances or house buildings, Charles Ingalls was an important guest. With other fiddlers and banjo players, or alone on his own violin, he'd play "The Irish Washerwoman," "Buffalo Gals," "The Money Musk" or "Sweet Betsy from Pike" for the dancers. At one of the parties, the snow fell so thickly in the Wisconsin woods that the guests could not leave for home. They didn't mind; they simply kept the fires burning and the candles lit and danced all night to the sound of Charles' fiddle.

On the other side of the Oconomowoc River from the Ingalls farm lived a family of Quiners and Holbrooks. The Ingalls and the Quiner children all became friends while they were growing up. Like the Ingallses, the Quiners came from the east. They had been among the first pioneer families to settle in the vicinity of Milwaukee, Wisconsin. The parents, Henry and Charlotte Quiner, had married in New Haven, Connecticut, in 1831, but they had lived in Ohio and Indiana before they settled in the Wisconsin woods. When their daughter Caroline was born on December 12, 1839, some said she was the first non-Indian baby born in the Milwaukee area.

In addition to Caroline, there were two Quiner boys, Joseph and Henry, and a sister named Martha. Later, Eliza and Thomas were born. Father Quiner did a lively business as a trader with the many Indians who still lived in the Wisconsin woods. The Indians often ventured into the settlement, to see what traders like Henry Quiner would give them for their animal skins and furs.

During the autumn of 1844, Father Quiner left home on a trading trip by sailing schooner on Lake Michigan. As the ship neared the Mackinac Straits, a violent lake storm blew up. Ship, crew and passengers were lost in the cold waters, including Father Quiner. Caroline was five that fall, but she always remembered the wagonload of relatives who came to tell her mother and brothers and sisters that their father was not coming home.

Without a father, life for the Quiners became bleak and sparse. Some friendly Indians helped feed the family through the first lonely winter; they remembered their fair trades with Henry Quiner. But food and fuel were often nearly gone. Once, flour for bread making ran out, and there was no money to buy more. The Quiners never forgot the generous man headed for Milwaukee who left a whole barrel of flour for the hungry family of seven.

In 1847, Mrs. Quiner decided that her children would fare better by living on a farm. The family moved to a piece of land along the Oconomowoc River, just a few miles from the village of Concord. On their farm, the Quiners raised bees for honey; they had chickens for eggs and cows for milk and butter. The garden and crops helped to feed the family.

In 1848, Mrs. Quiner married a farmer from Connecticut named Frederick Holbrook. Life became easier for the Quiner children. Their new stepfather purchased land next to the Quiner farm, making more space for animals to graze and crops to grow. In 1854, another sister was born; they named her Charlotte, after her mother, but called her Lottie.

Caroline Quiner wanted to teach; her mother had been educated in a "female seminary" back in Boston, and she taught before she married. So Caroline and her brothers and sisters often heard about the importance of education, even on the edge of the wild frontier. Caroline loved to read and learn, and to express her thoughts in poetry and written compositions that won praise from the teacher who boarded at the Quiner-Holbrook home.

When she finished her own schooling at age six-teen, Caroline passed the examination for her first teaching certificate. She was given a contract to teach at the same school she and her brothers and sisters had attended. Wages were low in 1856: her sister Martha remembered that Caroline taught for $2.50 or $3.00 per week. But the money was the first she had earned, and Caroline was proud of the clothes she bought, and of the wages she gave to her parents.

As a teacher, and as a young pioneer woman, Caroline was capable and steadfast and firm. She was often very quiet, but she was gentle and "proud and particular in all matters of good breeding," as her daughter Laura recalled. All these qualities were admired by the brown-bearded neighbor-boy–fiddler named Charles Ingalls. They met at parties and dances and at Sunday school and church; they roamed the nearby woods together and walked along the Oconomowoc River. After she had com-pleted her second term of school teaching, Caroline said yes when Charles asked her to marry him.

On February 1, 1860, Charles and Caroline stood before Reverend Lyman in the town of Concord and were married. It was the second time a Quiner had married an Ingalls. Two years before, Caroline's brother Henry had married Charles' sister Polly. And a year later, Caroline's sister Eliza married Charles' brother Peter.

Charles and Caroline's wedding tintype, taken at the time of their marriage, was carefully cherished through their life together. Then it was passed down to their daughter Laura. In the picture, they sat close together, with Charles' arm protectively around his bride. Their eyes were bright and luminous. They were a pioneer couple, well suited to life on the frontier and eager for adventures together. Caroline understood that Charles had a restless nature and a need to move on. Wherever they would be, Caroline knew how to create a home.

Their first journey away from home and family was in 1863. Charles' parents and some of his sisters and brothers moved north into the Big Woods of Wisconsin. They settled near the town of Pepin, a log cabin village on the shores of Lake Pepin. Actually, the lake was a wide spot of the Mississippi River that stretched three miles from the Wisconsin shore to the Minnesota bluffs on the other side.

Seven miles inland from Lake Pepin, Charles

and Caroline bought an eighty-acre piece of land together with Henry and Polly Quiner. It was good to have family close by in the Big Woods. Neighbors were few, and hard work sometimes required two men. Charles Ingalls and Henry Quiner were a sturdy team. They built two log houses; they worked together at clearing the land and harvesting crops; they roamed the woods, hunting, trapping and fishing side by side.

With neighbors so scarce in the Big Woods, and Henry and Polly's cabin so close, Charles and Caroline often visited. Their cabin was quiet, with no children, but the Quiner house, with three children, Louisa, Charley and Albert, was lively. The grownups often sat discussing the Civil War and its battles in faraway places like Gettysburg, Vicksburg and Atlanta. They talked of what President Lincoln said in Washington, and worried about Charles and Polly's two brothers, George and Hiram, who were off fighting for the Union. Sadly, Henry and Caroline's brother Joseph died from his wounds in the battle of Shiloh in 1862.

But the war seemed far away from the quiet, busy lives of pioneers in the Big Woods. Their days were filled with caring for farm animals, tending gardens and crops, keeping house and storing away wood and food for the long, cold wintertime. Pepin was seven miles away through the forest; it was too far to visit often. Rare trips were made to the town on the edge of the Mississippi but only for important business—for trading furs or stocking up on supplies from the stores.

On January 10, 1865, just as the Civil War was being concluded far beyond the Wisconsin woods, a baby girl was born in the Ingalls cabin. She was blue eyed and golden haired, and Charles and Caroline named her Mary Amelia. Two years later they become Pa and Ma to another girl baby, named Laura for Charles' mother.

In the center of the family Bible was a page to record births. In her careful handwriting, Ma had penned in her first baby's name and birthday:

Mary Amelia Ingalls born Tuesday, Jan. 10th 1865, Town, Pepin, Pepin Co., Wisconsin.

Now Ma added a second entry:

Laura Elizabeth Ingalls born Thursday, Feb. 7th 1867, Town, Pepin, Pepin Co., Wisconsin.

Laura's first memories were of the cabin in the

woods, her parents and her sister, Mary. In the evenings, after supper, the sound of Pa's fiddle became as regular as sunset to Laura's ears. "Auld Lang Syne," "Kitty Wells," "Annie Laurie," "Bonny Doon" and "Home Sweet Home" were some of the songs that lulled Laura and Mary to sleep. Often, the deep, mellow sound of Pa's voice joined the song of his fiddle.

The early memories of home were images that Laura always loved to recall. Later in her life she began calling them "the pictures that hang in my memory." The snug, cozy feeling of warm evenings, the voices of Pa and Ma and the soft firelight on the log walls made pictures that never faded for her.

"The first remembrance is of my Father always," she wrote. "My first memory is of his eyes, so clear and sharp and blue. Those eyes that could look so unerringly along a rifle barrel in the face of a bear or pack of wolves and yet were so tender as they rested on his Caroline, my mother, or me when I was sick. . . . His hair was thick and fine and he wore a tawny beard. He was the swiftest skater in the neighborhood, a strong swimmer and could travel miles on his snow shoes or tramp all day long through the woods. . . . His arms were so strong . . .

and they carried me many a night when I was sick and restless. I can hear his measured steps yet, back and forth across the floor, feel the comfort of those strong arms and hear his soothing, 'There, there.' And also his kind voice saying, 'Now Caroline, you lie down and sleep.'"

While Laura recalled Pa as strong and fearless and jolly, Ma was gentle and quiet and comforting as she went about her work in the cabin. "Lessons learned at Mother's knee last all through life," Laura said. "But dearer than Mother's teachings are little personal memories: Mother's face, Mother's touch, Mother's voice."

In the evenings, as Laura and Mary fell asleep in their trundle bed, they often heard Ma singing to them:

> Hush my babe, lie still and slumber,
>   Holy angels guard thy bed,
> Heavenly blessings without number
>   Gently resting on thy head.

Life on their Wisconsin farm was a comfortable one for Pa and Ma and Mary and Laura. Wood for fuel was everywhere, and Pa cut many cords of logs for burning through the snowy winters. He hunted and trapped, trading the furs of mink, muskrat, silver fox and bear for supplies in the village of Pepin. The wild game he shot provided fresh meat and salted meat for the cold months. Laura wrote that "I remember seeing deer that father had killed hanging in trees around our forest home." The venison meat was smoked and cured and stored in the attic of the cabin for winter meals.

During the summers, Pa worked hard tending crops, helping Uncle Henry and the other neighbors with their work, and clearing away the big woods to make fields and grazing places for his cows. It tired Pa, and annoyed him too, that he fought an everlasting battle with the forest. The trees always seemed determined to overtake the cleared fields.

Pa yearned for something the Big Woods of Wisconsin could never provide: the open prairie land he'd known as a boy in Illinois. There, a plow would sink into the rich black soil without a tree or stone in its way. Pa had heard that the plains of Kansas were open lands, ready for settlers. And Kansas was where he wanted to go.

2. Indian Territory

Our Uncle Sam is rich enough
To give us all a farm!

Those words made Pa Ingalls happy. He and Ma had worked hard to pay for their Wisconsin land, but in a depression following the Civil War, all their money had been lost in a bank failure. The idea of 160 acres of free government land on the prairie made Pa eager to go west. He wanted to stake his claim on land that the government was giving away to farmers.

"That's the ticket!" he'd exclaim when he thought about following the sunset west into new country.

The Big Woods was filling up with people. From settlements like Pepin and others along the Mississippi River, farmers were penetrating the forests. They were establishing new homes and farms, just as Pa and Ma had done.

By the late 1860's there were many Swedish neighbors living near the Ingalls farm. Ma enjoyed having people nearby, but they interfered with Pa's hunting and trapping. He knew that in the West, deer, antelope, prairie chickens and wild turkeys ran thick and free over the level land.

In the evenings, around the fireplace, Pa and Ma talked about moving west. They always discussed their plans together carefully. Pa was ready to leave Wisconsin, but Ma looked around her snug house, and at Mary and Laura, who were so young, and she wondered why they should leave home behind. Pa always remembered that Ma had been a teacher, and he said she had a way with words. As a schoolgirl, she had written a composition about her feelings for home and family. "Who would wish to leave home and wander forth, in the world, to meet its tempests and its storms?" Ma had written. "Give me a place at home, with a seat at the fireside, where all is happy and free."

But, as Laura once said, "My parents possessed the spirit of the frontier to a marked degree." They decided to follow the tradition of their families and move west. In 1868, Pa and Ma sold their farm to a Swedish settler named Gustaf Gustafson. Their destination was Kansas.

To prepare for the long trip from Wisconsin to Kansas, Pa fitted white, waterproof canvas over curving bows to cover his wagon. That covered wagon would be the family's home until they could build another house. Ma packed all the belongings from the little house that would fit in the wagon. Carefully, she wrapped the books she liked to read aloud to Pa, their clothes, dishes, bedding and keepsakes. Pa's fiddle rested softly between the quilts. It traveled with them like a friendly member of the family. Jack, the bulldog with dark spots on his tawny coat, would follow the wagon west. It was important to have a good watchdog on a trip into the wild, untamed territory.

Laura and Mary watched the preparations for moving, but they were too young to help. Family and friends wished the Ingallses good fortune on their journey, although many of Pa's and Ma's brothers and sisters wondered why they were leaving. The Big Woods were good enough for them!

On the day they left Wisconsin, Pa drove the horse-drawn covered wagon through the Big

Woods to the shores of Lake Pepin. There was thick ice on the lake, so it became a bridge to the West as Pa and his girls crossed over it. On the other side was the state of Minnesota.

The long journey west took the Ingalls family across Minnesota, south through Iowa and Missouri and finally, west into the state of Kansas. Laura told of that trip in her book *Little House on the Prairie*. Although she was too young to remember those experiences, Pa and Ma and Mary told her about it later.

"We rode in the covered wagon all day long, every day," Laura said. "We couldn't remember how many days it had been, for we were such little girls. We had seen strange woods and hills and creeks and rivers. We had crossed long bridges and been on ferry boats and for days we had been going along flat lands, covered with tall green grass where rabbits hid when they saw the wagon, and prairie chickens scuttled across the road."

The days of travel were not always easy ones. There were dangerous deep rivers and streams to cross and lonely times of driving for miles without seeing another human being. Sometimes the rains and hot sun made the wagon a miserable home. But because of Pa and Ma, Mary and Laura felt the wagon was homelike. Ma cooked good meals over the campfire when they stopped for the night. And Pa played his fiddle merrily, driving back the eerie sounds of the nighttime. His rifle was always in the wagon to keep them safe.

Pa drove the wagon to the southern part of Kansas and then veered west. He rejoiced that the land was level and treeless. There were nothing but grassy plains under the sky, which curved like a blue bowl over the wagon.

The Ingalls family came to the Verdigris River. The horses pulled the loaded wagon across the river, and Pa stopped them in the new frontier town called Independence. But Pa saw no need to stay long; he wanted the open prairie. The last stretch of the long journey continued another thirteen miles southwest of Independence.

Pa called the land above the Verdigris River bluffs the "high prairie." A stream called Walnut Creek broke the monotony of that flat stretch of land, and trees grew along its banks. Water and wood were important for a pioneer. In the distance, blue-green bluffs rose up from the prairie.

There was nothing to distinguish one rolling

plain from another on the high prairie. The sea of grass was level and empty-looking in all directions. There was no one to ask for advice about the place where the covered wagon stopped. Pa just said to Ma, "Here's the place we've been looking for."

The location where Pa and Ma decided to stop was in Rutland Township, in Montgomery County, Kansas. This Pa and Ma knew, but what they didn't know was that they had picked a place on land not legally open for settlers to homestead. They had driven three miles into what was called the Osage Diminished Reserve, a reservation set aside for the Indians. It was the home of the seven bands of Osage Indians.

The Osage Indians had lived along the Osage River in Missouri during the early 1800's. When settlers started moving into their Missouri hunting grounds, they were willing to give up their land and move west. In the 1860's, their reservation included all of Montgomery County, with the exception of a three-mile slice of land. The tribes lived in camps along the Verdigris, except while they were on hunting trips farther west. During one of those trips, settlers like the Ingalls family entered the quiet, empty lands and started building homes.

Pa did not bother to file a claim on the land; if he had, he would have found that he and his family were living on the Osage reserve. The prairie was so vast, and Pa was so anxious to build a house and start a farm, that he was not concerned with the business of applications for homestead land. His goal was to haul enough logs from the banks of Walnut Creek to construct a cabin.

Establishing a new home on the prairie was a difficult process. Pa had to select and cut straight trees for logs, bring them to the house site, and slowly raise the walls. A well was dug for fresh water, and a log stable was built to keep the horses safe from the wolves that still roamed the prairie.

On his hunting trips across the prairie, Pa encountered other new settlers. Some were frontiersmen, including a man Pa simply called Edwards. Pa met the Scott family, and he learned of Dr. George Tann, a black doctor who helped the Osages through sicknesses. Pa found them all to be "nice folks."

Charles Ingalls was a good carpenter, and he exchanged work with the neighbors, as pioneers often did. But Pa worked alone with his sod plow when he broke up the grasslands into fields. Breaking the prairie for the first time was hard labor for the man behind the plow and for the horses pulling it. The tall grass country was not used to the steel edge of the plow cutting the sod and turning the grass under. Sometimes the dense root system under the grass was so thick that Pa had to attack it with his ax before the plow could pass through.

Laura was three and a half in August of 1870, and she well remembered a trip she and Mary and Pa took across the prairie one hot summer day. Mrs. Scott, their jolly neighbor lady, had come to visit Ma, and they stayed in the shady cabin. Pa wanted his girls to see an Indian camp. Along with Jack, they walked across the prairie until they reached a little hidden valley.

The Osage were away on a hunting trip, so their camp was deserted, but Pa showed Mary and Laura the ashes where fires had been, and holes where tent poles had been sunk. In the dusty ground were bright spots of blue and red and green Indian beads. Mary and Laura hunted them for hours, with Pa helping. When the summer sun was setting, Pa and his girls walked home to the cabin on the high prairie.

They had left Mrs. Scott and Ma visiting together, but when they got home, Ma was lying in bed dozing. In the crook of her arm was a tiny, black-haired baby.

Ma told Mary and Laura that this was their baby sister. Pa said they would name her Caroline, after Ma, but they could call her Carrie. In the family Bible, Ma wrote:

Caroline Celestia Ingalls born Wednesday,
Aug. 3rd, 1870, Montgomery Co., Kansas.

Not long after baby Carrie was born, a visitor called at the Ingalls home—the United States census taker. The census was taken every ten years, whether people lived in Wisconsin or Kansas or Maine or California. Although the census taker spelled the family name as "Ingles," the rest of his listing was correct. He recorded that Pa, "C. P. Ingles," was a thirty-four-year-old carpenter. Ma was thirty and listed as "Keeping House." Mary was five, Laura was three, and Carrie was only two weeks old.

The census taker did not list a value on Pa's new farm, nor those of the neighbors nearby. The reason was that the settlers held no ownership of the land. The land still belonged to the Osage Indians.

Indians often stopped at the Ingalls cabin. They appeared as suddenly as rabbits or prairie chickens coming out of the prairie grass. Pa had unknowingly built the cabin along a dim old Indian trail, which was still used by the Osage. Sometimes, without a sound, Indian braves popped in through the low doorway. Like all visitors, they could be friendly or unfriendly, welcome or troublesome. Most of them were hungry. Ma gave them corn bread, and usually they left satisfied. Ma complained when the Indians visited while they were wearing smelly skunk skins.

Pa encountered Indians while he hunted, and they seemed friendly enough, although he and they could not communicate. But as more white-topped covered wagons drove into their land, and acres of grass were plowed up, the Osage could see that their hunting lands were being disturbed. The lands promised them by the United States government were being invaded. Their trails had been destroyed by log cabins and barns, and as had happened before, the wild animals the Indians hunted for food were being driven away.

Rumors passed from one prairie cabin to the next, saying that the Indians were angry. The government sent army cavalry to patrol the prairie.

Some claimed that the settlers, not the Osages, would be told to leave the area. Pa and Ma tried to ignore the stories, and they thought of the crops they would plant on the land Pa had plowed.

Finally, the Indians could no longer be ignored. In their camps in the valleys, the bands of Osage debated war against the farmers, to protect their lands. Peaceful nights in the Ingalls cabin turned to nightmarish hours of fear as the sound of the Indians' angry chanting and war whoops replaced the peaceful music of Pa's fiddle. "It was far more terrifying a sound than the howling of wolves," Laura said. She remembered those howling screams all her life, but also that Pa stood sentinel with his gun, protecting the family.

Congress wanted to offer the Osage tribe 18 cents an acre for their land so that a railroad could be built. President Grant refused to allow a sale that gave the Indians such a small sum in exchange for asking them to leave. In 1870, the United States Congress voted to pay the Osage $1.25 per acre for their Kansas land, and to give them a new reservation in Oklahoma. These decisions in far-off Washington were what caused the Osage councils to argue so hotly during nights of debate.

The Indians decided to accept the offer. When they left on the fall hunt, they rode across the old trail that passed right by the Ingalls cabin. Pa and Ma, Mary, Laura and Carrie were all there when the long, long line of Indians on foot and on horseback went on to yet another reservation.

The Indians were not the only people who left Montgomery County. Some of the settlers moved on, too. The Indians' future had been decided by a treaty with Washington; a letter from Wisconsin helped the Ingalls family to decide theirs. The letter was from Gustaf Gustafson, who had bought Pa's farm near Pepin. He did not want to finish paying for the land, and he wanted Pa to take it back.

Pa and Ma discussed returning to Wisconsin. They decided to go. Ma mourned all the work and time they lost by leaving their prairie home behind. It seemed all for nothing. But Pa was not concerned.

"Never mind, Caroline," he said. "Wisconsin is not so bad. There will be good fishing in Lake Pepin and hunting in the Big Woods. There'll be strawberries on the hill slopes—and sprouts in the wheat field, but what're a few sprouts more or less?"

3. "Give Them a Covered Wagon and They're Ready to Go!"

The long journey from Kansas back to the Big Woods in Wisconsin took many weeks. Laura was four during that spring of 1871. When at last Pa drove the horses and the covered wagon into the clearing where their cabin stood, Laura could see someone else's smoke curling up from the chimney. The Gustafsons still lived in the house where Laura had been born. But they planned to leave for the West, and then the Ingalls family could settle into their old home.

Uncle Henry and Aunt Polly Quiner still lived close by. They invited Pa and Ma and their girls to stay until the Gustafsons were gone. It was a crowded, jolly time for the two families. Mary and Laura and Carrie were pleased to have their four cousins as playmates. They got well acquainted with their cousins Louisa, Charley, Albert and Lottie.

All the Wisconsin relatives were happy to have this Ingalls family back home in the Big Woods. Uncle Peter and Aunt Eliza came visiting, bringing cousins Peter, Alice, Ella and Edith. Ma's brother Tom Quiner came walking out of the woods with presents for the girls. Pa's parents, Grandpa and Grandma Ingalls, were glad to see them. All the relatives listened to Pa's exciting tales of Indian Territory. He was a good storyteller.

When the Ingalls family moved back to their cabin in the Big Woods, Pa once again started farming the cleared fields in the forest. The passing seasons—the long winters, the springtime woods, the growing seasons of summer and the harvesttimes of autumn—were carefully stored up in Laura's memory. Those times were written about many years later in her first book, *Little House in the Big Woods.*

After the Wisconsin homecoming, Laura made her first discovery of books and reading. A half mile down the road from the Ingalls cabin was the Barry Corner School. Mary was six and old enough to enroll for the springtime term of 1871. With the Quiner cousins, she walked to school and back. Laura was lonely but waited eagerly for Mary to teach her what she had learned each day. While Ma cooked supper, Mary showed Laura the words she had learned, so Laura could read almost as soon as Mary could.

Both Pa and Ma valued books. In the evenings, if Pa was not playing the fiddle or telling the girls one of his own stories, Ma read aloud to him. She read the novels *Norwood* and *Millbank*; she read *General Ben Butler of New Orleans* and a volume about Jerusalem, *The Land and the Book*. Listening to Ma read helped awaken Laura's lifelong fascination with words.

Many years after those reading sessions in the Big Woods, Laura was asked how she had developed her skill as a writer. She replied that her early exposure to books had taught her the importance of reading and writing. "Pa and Ma were great readers," Laura said, "and I read a lot at home with them."

When the fall term of school started in October of 1871, Laura went along with Mary. The girls swung a shiny new dinner pail between them and took turns carrying their one schoolbook. Laura was not yet five, but she thought spending the day at school was wonderful. Besides Mary and her cousins, Laura's playmate Clarence Huleatt was there. Laura and Mary knew the Huleatt children, Clarence and Eva. Pa and Ma were good friends of their parents. The Huleatt farm was just a mile from the Ingalls cabin. The two families often visited back and forth.

The neighborhood surrounding the Ingalls farm was so thickly settled that company often stopped to visit Pa and Ma. Dances were popular pastimes, and Pa's fiddling again added to the music. Laura loved watching the dancers take over the floor when the fiddlers began. She stood with other little children, watching the ladies' full skirts and the men's boots going by as the music played and the caller shouted the dance steps.

For two seasons, Pa farmed his clearing in the Wisconsin woods. He still grumbled about the sprouting trees that constantly rooted in his cleared fields. Pa wanted to go west again. He had liked the Kansas plains, and he wanted once again to live on the prairie. His fiddle even sang of far-off places. Pa played "Old Folks at Home," "Dixie" and "There is a Happy Land." Pa's voice was full of longing when he sang, "In the starlight, in the starlight, Let us wander gay and free."

Ma laughed when Pa talked to her so earnestly about moving west again. She said that all Pa had was an itching foot. Trees and hills and neighbors suited Ma much better than the bare, flat, lonely plains.

Pa talked to Uncle Peter and Aunt Eliza about moving west across the Mississippi River to the state of Minnesota. Beyond the bluffs and the round wooded hills of the river bottoms, the prairies flattened out past towns like Mankato and New Ulm. Ma liked the idea of traveling with another family over those flat lands with so few towns and settlers.

For the second time, Pa sold his farm in the Big Woods. Late in the fall of 1873, a Swedish farmer named Anderson bought the place for $1,000. Until the time came to go west, Pa and Ma and the girls stayed with Uncle Peter and Aunt Eliza. Mary and Laura attended school with their cousins, walking through the snow to the log schoolhouse. But school days were few; the adults were eager to start the trip west. The wagons must cross Lake Pepin before the ice became thin and soft. Sometimes people waited too long, and their loaded wagons went crashing through the ice into the deep, cold waters.

Early in February 1874, the two Ingalls families, Pa's and Uncle Peter's, were ready to leave for Minnesota. Grandma and Grandpa Ingalls, aunts, uncles, cousins and friends all stood around watching them go. It was so cold and the wind blew across the ice of Lake Pepin so bitterly that no one wanted the families to leave the warm firesides of their cabins in the woods. Most of Pa's and Ma's brothers and sisters never moved farther west than their Wisconsin homes. One uncle, wondering why anyone would want to venture out into the unknown, tried to explain the pioneering wanderlust of Charles and Peter Ingalls. "Give them a covered wagon," he exclaimed, "and they're ready to go!"

On February 7, 1874, Laura's seventh birthday, the families crossed Lake Pepin. On the other side was the town of Lake City, Minnesota. Pa and Ma and Uncle Peter and Aunt Eliza bustled all the cousins into the warmth of the Lake City hotel. Pa vanished, then came back bringing Laura a birthday present. It was a book of poems called *The Floweret.*

Lake City was on the eastern edge of Minnesota, but Pa wanted to settle in the western part of the state. February and March were too cold to drive so far in the wagons, so Pa and Uncle Peter found an abandoned cabin where the families camped together until the weather was warmer. Uncle Peter located a farm along the Zumbro River where he wanted to settle, so when the time came to travel on, Pa and Ma, Mary, Laura and Carrie drove west alone.

One night on the journey across Minnesota, Laura was falling asleep in the wagon when she heard what she said was a "clear, wonderful call." Ma told her it was the whistle of a railroad train. Looking out into the darkness from the shelter of the wagon, Laura saw a speeding train for the first time.

"We were all silent, watching till the train was out of sight," Laura recalled. "Then Pa said we were living in a great age. He said that in a day a train covered more distance than an ox team could travel in a week, and he spoke of railroads conquering the Great American Desert."

Day after day, the Ingalls wagon moved west. The springtime prairie was green with grasses and colored with wildflowers. They saw few people, but Laura loved the long days of driving along the prairie trails. The fresh air blew through the canvas-covered wagon, and Mary and Laura and Carrie played quietly behind Pa and Ma, who rode on the high wagon seat. Pa picked beautiful little nooks along prairie creeks for camping spots. At the end of the day, he built a fire, and Ma cooked supper over the flames. Laura was old enough to help Ma, but she was too short to reach the camp table where Ma prepared the meals. She stood on a wooden box to wash the dishes with Mary after supper.

All along the way west, Pa played his fiddle as they sat around the campfire. He was content on the prairie, and was always happy to be moving to new, unseen places. Laura felt the same way.

One day, Pa drove the wagon into a little village called Walnut Grove. There were just a few stores and houses scattered around the railroad tracks on the prairie. When the Ingalls family first saw the town it was only three years old. But out on the surrounding prairies, newcomers were already establishing farms.

In Walnut Grove, Pa learned that a Norwegian settler who lived a mile north of town wanted to move away. He was willing to let Pa buy his home-stead. It consisted of 172 acres of prairie soil, along a stream called Plum Creek. There was a house there, a dugout. On the tall creek bank, the little house was dug into the ground, with thick sod walls. The roof was made of willow boughs, with lengths of sod laid over them thickly. Grass grew on the roof, and except for the stovepipe sticking up, it looked exactly like the rest of the prairie ground.

The dugout house was small; there was just one room, about the size of the wagon. But Pa and Ma knew it would be cool in summer and snug in win-ter. From the dugout's door, they could look across the creek to the great sweep of level prairie land. Pa said he would never feel crowded in such wide-open country. He planned to raise acres of wheat on his farm, and with Walnut Grove and the railroad so near, the grain could be shipped by train to the big flour mills in St. Paul. Prospects were good in the new home on the Minnesota prairie.

In the evenings, Pa liked to sit just outside the dugout door as the sun set, looking over the new land. His voice and the fiddle sang together:

> "Home, home, sweet, sweet home.
> Be it ever so humble,
> There's no place like home."

4. Along Plum Creek

Laura and Mary played along Plum Creek nearly every day during the first spring and summer they lived in the dugout. They wandered far up the stream, exploring under the shady willow trees and playing on the gravely beach. Their toes squished through the mud on the wet creek bank, and the girls hid in the thickets of wild plums. Sometimes they went fishing, bringing back their catch for Ma to fry for supper.

Over Plum Creek's high bank lay the endless prairie. The girls wandered over Pa and Ma's new land, following the birds and butterflies and picking grass flowers. They could see Pa in the distance, working with his plow and ox team, turning up the sod for wheat fields. He told the girls that their bumper crops would make them rich!

Ma kept house in the dugout, keeping it comfortable and homey. She expected her girls to help her; each morning Laura brought water for the day. Both she and Mary played with Carrie. They washed dishes and set the table. On certain afternoons, they sat quietly and worked at their sewing. Laura much preferred being out in the sun and wind, but patiently she sewed during the quiet hours in the dugout. Laura learned discipline on those days, and that there was satisfaction in a job well done.

With the town of Walnut Grove so close, there were opportunities for the civilized living Ma had missed while living so deep in the Big Woods and in Indian Territory. During the summer of 1874, Pa and Ma helped to organize the Union Congregational Church. The Home Missionary Society in Boston sent out traveling ministers to new frontier territories, and the Reverend Edward Alden was assigned to help Walnut Grove start a church. The building of the church started almost immediately after the first organized meeting.

With so many families arriving in Walnut Grove, a school was started. Pa and Ma were eager for their girls to have an education. When Laura first heard that she and Mary would be going to school, she had a jittery feeling of fear. She dreaded meeting so many strangers. "We were just two wild Indians, seven and nine years old, and on our own for the first time," Laura said of the day they started school. She was sure she preferred running wild and free on the prairie along Plum Creek.

At school, Mary and Laura learned quickly. They studied from Ma's old schoolbooks. All the students had different books, brought from their homes in the east. Surprisingly, this did not matter. As Laura said, "A sum is a sum, no matter what the name of the arithmetic book."

The Ingalls girls grew to like their school days. Laura looked forward to recess time, when the children ran and played and joined in games like ante-over and Uncle John. Most of the students were sons and daughters of homesteaders, like Laura. There were only a few town children, like Nellie and Willie Owens. The Owenses lived behind their parents' store on the dusty main street of Walnut Grove. They were loud and spoiled and mean to other children.

When Laura wrote of these times in her book

On the Banks of Plum Creek, she renamed the Owens family Oleson. In all her writing, Laura used the real names of her characters with two exceptions. In these two cases, she chose not to identify their real names because they were such unpleasant people.

Laura watched the building of the Congregational church as she walked to and from school with Mary. Finally, the pioneer church was complete. On Sundays, the Ingalls family, dressed in their best, rode to church in the wagon. Mary and Laura went to Sunday school with many of their classmates. They sang together and learned the Bible verses. Since Laura loved to read, she eagerly borrowed books from the small Sunday school library.

The minister, Reverend Alden, traveled to many churches in Minnesota. Sundays when he could be in Walnut Grove were special. Pa and Ma became very fond of the minister, who affectionately called Mary, Laura and Carrie his "country girls." When Reverend Alden mentioned that money was needed to buy a church bell, Pa responded generously. He contributed $26.15 to the church bell fund. When the bell was installed, its clanging chimes could be heard on the Ingalls farm.

Laura always remembered the Christmas celebration at the new church on December 20, 1874.
The whole town seemed to be there. Together the
pioneers in the new land celebrated a happy Christmas. The centerpiece of it all was the Christmas
tree, the first one Laura had ever seen. There were
presents for everyone on the tree. Laura was thrilled
with the fur cape and muff and little china jewel box
that she received.

Soon after Christmas, the Ingalls family learned
what a northern prairie winter was like. Minnesota
was blizzard country, and there was nothing on the
open land to stop the wind. It blew furiously, mixed
with snow and sleet, until seeing became impossible. Stories circulated about people lost in blizzards
and frozen to death a few steps from their doors.
Cattle sometimes wandered loose and helpless and
were found miles away. Pa soon learned to have
plenty of wood handy during a winter blow. Blizzards often raged for three or four days, keeping everyone snowbound. The trains along the railroad
would be stalled until the tracks were cleared of
snowdrifts.

During the blizzard season, Mary and Laura did

not go to school. Ma taught them at home. It was risky for anyone to leave shelter for long. "The blizzards," Laura explained, "always came quick enough to catch people unprepared. No one measured the speed of wind in those days, but it surely was as fast as hurricane speed. Whichever way one went into the blizzard, he went against it."

Big snows on the prairie usually meant enough moisture to grow good crops the following summer. Pa was so exuberant about the promise of a wheat crop that during the spring of 1875 he built a new house for his family. The wheat crop was bright green in the fields when Pa drove into Walnut Grove with the wagon and returned with a load of yellow pine lumber, which had been shipped by train to the treeless prairie. He also bought glass windows, factory-milled doors and white china doorknobs. Pa had purchased it all on credit at the lumberyard. Everyone in Walnut Grove knew about his big wheat fields and trusted him to pay the bills at harvesttime.

Laura and Mary watched the building of the new house with excitement. Their neighbor, a Norwegian named Eleck Nelson, helped Pa frame the house, roof it, hang the doors and windows and nail the narrow siding to the walls. When the house was done, it was yellow and new on the green land. The house stood on the creek bank opposite the dugout, nearer to the road to town.

Laura called the new home "the wonderful house." Inside, on moving day, there was a surprise for Ma. It was a shiny, black iron cookstove.

When they moved into the new house and watched the wheat growing so well, Laura said that her entire family had the feeling that "it was a good world." Each summer day was busy, working the fast-growing vegetable garden, taking the cow to graze on the prairie and playing along Plum Creek. But a terrible day came to change all the hopes and dreams of Pa and Ma for their prairie farm. It was the day of the grasshopper invasion.

Laura remembered the thick cloud of grasshoppers darkening the sun and descending on the prairie. Within minutes, there was the sound of hungry insects eating everything in sight. The wheat crop, the garden, the plum thicket and the waving grasses were devoured. Laura said that the Minnesota grasshopper summers were the worst since the ancient insect plagues in Egypt, described in the Bible.

"I have lived among uncounted millions of grasshoppers," Laura wrote later. "I saw their bodies choke Plum Creek. I saw them destroy every green thing on the face of the earth." The Minnesota farmers mourned their lost crops, and many of them simply left their land and moved away. Merchants in Walnut Grove wondered if they could keep their businesses open. The eaten, dry prairie became dusty and ugly with grasshoppers devouring anything they could forage.

Pa and Ma would not abandon their new farm. Pa decided to earn money in eastern Minnesota as a harvester. Crops were good there; he could work long days throughout the harvest season and earn wages.

Pa walked over two hundred miles across Minnesota before he found work. While he was gone, Laura and Mary bravely helped Ma with work around the farm. The Nelsons were good neighbors, and when Mr. Nelson went into Walnut Grove, he brought back letters from Pa. Pa's letters helped cheer his family from week to week.

The days dragged while Pa was away. There was

no cheery fiddle music in the evenings, no story-telling and joking. Pa's girls were lonely and miserable without him. It was a happy day when he came walking back to Plum Creek, with his pocket full of money he had earned. Once again, his laugh and his fiddling filled the house on Plum Creek.

Pa and Ma decided that they should move into Walnut Grove for the winter, so that Mary and Laura could safely go to school. It was too risky to walk from the farm on Plum Creek to town, when blizzards were so unpredictable. Pa found a little house for rent behind the church, and the family moved. The girls started back to school regularly during the fall of 1875.

Laura remembered coming home from school on November 1, 1875. A neighbor lady was busy getting supper, and Ma was in bed—with a new baby brother! He was named Charles Frederick Ingalls, after Pa and after Ma's stepfather. The girls soon started calling him Freddie. They hurried home after school each day to see their first brother. Everyone was very proud of the baby boy.

Through the winter in town, the family longed to go back home to the farm on Plum Creek. Early in the spring, when snow was still on the ground, they moved. When warm weather came, Pa sowed another wheat crop. He planted a small field, because he could not predict if the "pesky hoppers" would be around during the 1876 growing season.

The grasshoppers had laid eggs in the ground, and when they hatched, once again their feasting started. Grass, gardens, crops, leaves on trees and any green growth vanished from the land. Some hungry hoppers tried to eat the wash on the clotheslines and the paint on buildings. Pa was disgusted; he said they'd not remain in such a "blasted country." He wrote a letter to Uncle Peter and Aunt Eliza in eastern Minnesota, telling them of the hard times the grasshoppers had caused. Some folks in Walnut Grove were signing papers saying that they had no money at all. If they signed, the state would give them small supplies of flour, pork, matches and other necessities. Pa and Ma would have no part of taking charity.

People were leaving Walnut Grove. The Steadmans, who were friends from the church, decided to buy a hotel in a town called Burr Oak, Iowa. They asked Pa and Ma to move there and help them operate the hotel called the Burr Oak House. The work would start late in the fall.

Uncle Peter wrote and told Pa to bring the whole family to his farm; Pa could work in the fields before they left for Burr Oak. A new settler named Kellar offered to buy the house and farm along Plum Creek. The Ingalls family made preparations to go east, not west.

When life in the West became too difficult, pioneer families sometimes returned to their old homes. This was called "back-trailing." This is what the Ingalls family did by leaving Walnut Grove. Pa and Laura felt it keenly. "How I wished we were going west!" Laura exclaimed. "Pa did not like to turn his back on the West either."

5. A Year in Burr Oak

"Almost everyone we meet is crying hard times if they live where the Grasshoppers are," wrote Laura's Grandmother Holbrook. Grandma and the rest of the Quiner and Ingalls relatives were all concerned to hear that Charles and Caroline and their girls had no home. Although the families were widely separated, they learned news of each other through what they called the "circulator." It was a letter mailed from family to family. Each added news to the bottom of the letter, and passed it on. Grandma Holbrook wrote of Laura's family: "I wonder when they will get a stopping place? I shall be glad for their sake; they have had a hard time of it since they left Pepin."

When Pa drove the covered wagon into Uncle

Peter's yard near South Troy, Minnesota, Laura forgot for a moment the hardships of the long trip and the fact that baby Freddie was often sick. Again there were cousins to play with. Peter, Alice, Ella, Edith and Lansford were almost like brothers and sisters to Laura and Mary and Carrie. Since Aunt Eliza was Ma's sister, and Uncle Peter was Pa's brother, the children were all double cousins.

Uncle Peter and Aunt Eliza urged Pa and Ma to stay with them for the rest of the summer. They were not needed in Burr Oak until autumn. Together, the two families totaled thirteen people. With so many people in one house, there were many chores to do, and the children were kept busy. Mary and fourteen-year-old Alice worked along with Ma and Aunt Eliza, cooking and tending the babies, Freddie and Lansford. Laura, Ella and Peter were put in charge of the cows.

Laura loved the daily task of watching the cows and guarding the haystacks that Pa and Uncle Peter had made. The Zumbro River flowed along the edge of Uncle Peter's pasture, and Laura and the cousins explored its banks. As their bare feet padded through the soft, green grass, they were mindful of the tinkling cow bells and where the cows were. It would never do for a cow to wander off, or to tear down the hay being saved for winter.

Wild plums grew along the Zumbro River, just as they had on Plum Creek. When one of the cousins found a cluster of them deep in a plum thicket, he or she would yell, and the rest of the children would come clamoring for the juicy fruit. Sometimes they would light little fires and roast crabapples, or bits of bread and meat. As sunset neared, the cousins found the cows, or the cows found them, and they all went back to the stable for milking time.

Through the long summer days, Laura worried about baby Freddie. He was nine months old and sickly. Pa and Ma were so concerned that they had a doctor come to examine the baby. The weeks were shadowed by his illness. Laura remembered the "awful day"; it was August 27, 1876, when Freddie "straightened out his little body and was dead."

Not far from Uncle Peter's house, Charles Frederick Ingalls was buried under a little white gravestone. The sad days that followed were even sadder because Pa and Ma and the girls knew that soon they would have to leave Freddie behind, alone in

Charles and Caroline Ingalls posed for this photo
soon after their 1860 wedding.

(By permission of Laura Ingalls Wilder Home Association)

Carrie, Mary and Laura Ingalls, around 1880.
(By permission of Laura Ingalls Wilder Home Association)

Baby Grace Ingalls.

The Ingalls family posed
for this portrait before Laura
moved to Mansfield in 1894.
Standing: Carrie, Laura and
Grace. Seated: Ma, Pa, Mary.
(By permission of Laura Ingalls Wilder
Home Association)

Rose Wilder at age three, photographed in Spring Valley, Minnesota.
(By permission of Laura Ingalls Wilder Home Association)

Laura and Almanzo Wilder in De Smet, the winter after their marriage.
(By permission of Laura Ingalls Wilder Home Association)

Almanzo Wilder at work on Rocky Ridge Farm.
(By permission of Laura Ingalls Wilder Home Association)

Rose and her donkey, Spookendyke.
(By permission of Laura Ingalls Wilder Home Association)

The Wilder house in the village of Mansfield, 1907.
(By permission of Laura Ingalls Wilder Home Association)

The completed home on Rocky Ridge Farm, around 1913.
(Author's Collection)

the little graveyard. But they would never forget him.

The Minnesota autumn was cool and crisp when Pa and Ma loaded the wagon once again. It was time to meet their promise to be hotelkeepers in Burr Oak, Iowa. Saying good-bye to Uncle Peter's family, Pa drove the wagon south. They crossed the Minnesota state line into the state of Iowa; Burr Oak was just three miles away.

When Pa's wagon rumbled into the village of Burr Oak and drove down the long Main Street, Laura saw immediately that it was far different from the fresh, western newness of Walnut Grove. Burr Oak, Laura said, "was an old town, built of red brick. I liked a new town better and I knew Pa did, too."

At an earlier time, Burr Oak had been on the crossroads of the western movement. The road going north led to Minnesota. The trail from the banks of the Mississippi ran westward through Burr Oak across Iowa, Nebraska and all the way to the Pacific coast. Sometimes as many as two hundred covered wagons had stopped to spend the night in Burr Oak. The pioneers would camp in clusters among the tall oak groves or stop in the yards of the neat brick houses. There was a brick mill in the village, and a stone quarry nearby, so many of the buildings were constructed of stone or brick.

There were two hotels still doing business in Burr Oak when the Ingalls family arrived. The busiest was the American House; the stagecoach made its stops there. The other hotel was the Burr Oak House. Some called it the Masters Hotel, for its most recent owner had been William Masters. That was where Pa stopped the wagon. The hotel was the new home of the Ingalls family.

The Burr Oak House seemed very grand to Laura. It was built on a hill that sloped down to Silver Creek. The lower level of the hotel included the kitchen, the dining room and sleeping space. From the street, doors opened to the tavern room, the hotel office and the parlor. A big bedroom off the parlor was occupied by Mr. Bisbee, the richest boarder. Upstairs were four small sleeping rooms.

Behind the hotel was a barn and a springhouse built over a flowing brook. Laura was often called to fetch butter and milk from the springhouse, where it was kept ice-cold. A fishpond was in the yard, and Silver Creek angled across the lot, full of speckled trout. Laura described the Burr Oak House as all together "a very fine place."

The hotel was a busy establishment. Visitors constantly came and went and, three times a day, hungry guests lined the long dining tables in the lower level of the hotel. Dances and weddings sometimes were held there. Some people lived at the hotel permanently. They were called the "steady boarders" and were treated with extra care.

Mr. and Mrs. Steadman, with their three boys, Johnny, Ruben and Tommy, had already settled into the hotel when the Ingalls family arrived. It had been agreed that Pa and Ma would help operate the hotel with the Steadmans, in exchange for living space and a part of the profits.

Pa immediately became very busy, helping around the hotel. Ma worked hard with Mrs. Steadman and the hired girl, doing the cooking, cleaning and laundry. Mary and Laura made beds, washed dishes and waited on tables. Mrs. Steadman also begged the girls to watch her youngest boy, Tommy.

Amy, the hired girl, knew many stories about the people who had previously owned the hotel and about the guests, too. When Laura asked Amy about the hole in the dining-room door, she learned that it was a bullet hole. It had been made by the son of Mr. Masters, the former owner of the hotel. Will Masters' wife had been running from him because he was drunk. She had slammed the kitchen door, and Will had shot his gun right through it. "The bullet hole in the door was thrilling to us children," Laura said.

Pa and Ma were concerned when they saw that a saloon stood next door to the hotel. It was this very saloon that had tempted Will Masters. The reason his father had sold the hotel was to take Will far away from the saloon, out west to Walnut Grove.

The Burr Oak school was a brick building, with two rooms, not far from the hotel. Mary and Laura started attending, along with the Steadman boys. Perhaps Carrie enrolled too; she was past six. Miss Sarah Donlan was the teacher in the primary room. William Reid was the secondary teacher and principal. Laura knew him well, because he lived at the hotel.

Around Christmastime, a group of big, scuffling farm boys started coming to school—not to learn, but to be unruly and to drive Mr. Reid out of town. They boasted to the crowd in the saloon that Reid would be gone after Christmas. The worst of the boys was named Mose. He led the others in mischief and noise. When he walked into the schoolroom tardy, Mr. Reid quietly asked him to come to his desk.

Laura said the rest of the students sat spellbound, hoping that Mr. Reid would not get hurt. But quickly, as Mose approached the desk, Mr. Reid tripped him. Mose fell across the teacher's knees and was whipped soundly with a ruler. When Mr. Reid was through, Mose walked through the door and never returned. His friends also skulked away, and school went on peacefully.

Except for some sledding down the long hill behind the hotel, Christmas was not very happy for Laura. The family still missed Freddie, though Ma was expecting a new baby in the spring. The work in the hotel kept Pa and Ma too occupied to plan for holidays. Besides, there was no place in the crowded hotel to celebrate. And then the Ingalls girls and the Steadman boys all got the measles.

Laura knew that Pa and Ma were talking of leaving the hotel. But before that happened, Laura was forced to spend hours with the best-paying boarder in the hotel, Mr. Bisbee. He decided to teach Laura to sing, and every day she had to practice the musical scales he taught her. Over the sounds of the noisy hotel, Laura sang patiently, "Do, re, me, fa, sol, la, ti, do."

Pa and Ma found rooms to rent over the grocery store, two doors from the hotel, on the other side of the saloon. The family moved into the quiet, pleasant apartment for the rest of the winter. Pa worked at a mill, where farmers came to have their corn and wheat ground up. Pa's horses were hitched to a millstone and walked around in a circle, grinding the grain.

The Ingalls girls enjoyed school during the winter of 1877. Mary had received *The Independent Fifth Reader* for her twelfth birthday on January 10. The book contained wonderful, stirring poems, speeches and stories, such as "Paul Revere's Ride," "The Village Blacksmith," "Bears Out for a Holiday" and "Snow-Bound." Mr. Reid was an elocutionist who taught the girls how to read aloud with feeling and emotion. Laura said she was always grateful for this training. Pa told her later that a crowd of men used to gather in the grocery store just below the Ingalls sitting room to listen while she and Mary recited and practiced their reading lessons.

Pa and Ma's worries about the saloon next door came true late one night. It caught fire, and Ma awakened Mary and Laura and Carrie, telling them to dress quickly in case their place started burning too. Ma and the girls stood by the front windows, looking down at a group of Burr Oak men lined up in front of the town pump. They had started a bucket brigade to pass the filled pails down the line to be poured on the flames. But the line seemed to be standing still.

Ma kept saying, "Why don't they hurry!" Nothing moved. Finally, Pa gave a shout and jerked Mr. Bisbee away from the flowing pump. In his panic, he had been pumping water into a pail with no bottom, screaming "Fire!" but doing nothing to stop the blaze.

At last the saloon fire was put out. Pa came in tired and smoky and grumbling. He told the girls that if the darned saloon could have burned without taking the rest of Burr Oak, he would have let it happen. He wouldn't have carried one drop of water to save a wild saloon like that.

Pa and Ma didn't like their girls so near the saloon, so they rented a red brick house on the edge of Burr Oak from Mr. Bisbee, and the family moved again. The comfortable house stood near an oak woods, and everyone was happy to be there. Pa had bought a cow, and once again Laura had the job of taking the cow to the pasture in the morning and bringing her home at night. Laura was ten and had to wear shoes all day, but she always went barefoot to get the cow.

Springtime in Burr Oak was green and fresh and sweet smelling with the scent of wildflowers and newly plowed black fields. School started getting long and tedious, and Laura was happy when the end drew close. She had worked hard to learn her multiplication tables that year, and after many mistakes, she finally mastered them.

Laura was busy helping Ma that spring, because a new baby was soon to be born. "One day," Laura recalled, "when I came back from an errand that had taken me a long time, I found a new little sister. Her hair was golden like Mary's and her eyes were bright and blue like Pa's." The date was May 23,

1877, and the name Pa and Ma chose for their fourth daughter was Grace Pearl.

"That was a delightful summer," Laura remembered. "Work and play were so mixed that I could not tell them apart." Helping to tend Grace was fun, taking and bringing the cow marked mornings and evenings, and playing with Carrie and Mary and their friends kept Laura busy.

Pa worked all summer for whoever would hire him. He could help on farms or work as a carpenter, but his wages were not enough to support a big family of four growing girls. Laura was not surprised to hear him talk of going west again. The summer days were so long and happy, and the brick house was so comfortable, that Laura never thought her family was poor. But other people in Burr Oak did, and thought they could help Ma and Pa out by raising one of their girls.

Dr. and Mrs. Starr were among Burr Oak's most important citizens. They liked Laura very much, and one afternoon when she came in from bringing the cow home, Laura saw Mrs. Starr talking earnestly with Ma. She was saying that her girls, Ida and Fannie, were grown and away teaching, and she was lonely for a girl around her big house. She and the doctor had talked it over, and they wanted Pa and Ma to give them Laura for their own.

Ma listened politely, but much to Laura's great relief, she said that she and Pa could not possibly spare their Laura. Mrs. Starr went away very sad to her empty house. When Laura thought of her offer, and of life without her own family, she tried to forget Mrs. Starr's visit as quickly as she could.

Pa was restless, thinking of the West, and of how hard he had to work to stay in a place he did not like. His fiddle played marching, moving songs. He wanted to go west again, and he knew that Walnut Grove suited him better than Burr Oak. He sold the cow and covered the wagon once more.

Very early one cool autumn morning, before sunrise, Pa and Ma finished loading the wagon and helped their sleepy girls inside. Before the sun rose, they had driven the three miles to the Minnesota state line. Burr Oak was behind them, they were back in Minnesota and Pa turned the wagon west. "We were all so happy about going west again," Laura recalled.

Yes, the West was best. Laura thought of the past year as the wagon plodded on the way back to

Walnut Grove. They had lost Freddie but gained Grace. They had lived in many places, among many people. Pa had learned that an old, crowded place was not for him. "I *know* that Pa was happy," Laura said of their return to western Minnesota. "The fiddle music he played along the road west was rousing and rollicking. To the stars Pa played and sang, 'Marching Through Georgia,' 'The Star Spangled Banner,' 'Yankee Doodle' and 'The Arkansas Traveler.'"

To Laura, "Burr Oak seemed like a dream from which we had awakened."

6. Going West Again

"No one, who has not pioneered, can understand the fascination of it," Laura said when she tried to explain the reason that so many American families like her own responded to the lure of traveling west. It was odd, Laura mused, "because everything came at us out of the West . . . storms, blizzards, grasshoppers, burning hot winds and fires . . . yet it seemed that we wanted nothing so much as we wanted to keep going west!"

When the Ingalls family returned to Walnut Grove, in the fall of 1877, they were welcomed as though they had come home. They drove up to the Ensign home and were invited to stay, not just for the night, but until Pa could build a house for his family. The Ensigns were good friends of Pa and

Ma's, from the Congregational Church. Their children, Willard, Anna and Howard, had always played with Mary, Laura and Carrie. It was not uncommon for families to "double up" on the frontier. Everyone simply moved over and made room for each other and lived as one family.

The grasshopper years had run their course in Walnut Grove, and the town was growing. William Masters, who had once owned the Burr Oak House, had built a new hotel in Walnut Grove. A house had been built near the church for the minister, and the Reverend Leonard Moses was assigned to Walnut Grove permanently. The Reverend Edward Alden continued to do his missionary work, founding churches farther west where there were none.

Pa quickly found a job in a store and was often asked to do carpentry work around Walnut Grove. Ma helped Mrs. Ensign cook and clean for their big combined family, and she tended to Baby Grace. Mary, Laura and Carrie went to school each morning, along with the Ensign children. Laura remembered that "we all studied the same books, only I was at the beginning of the grammar, arithmetic, history and geography, while Mary was quite a ways farther over and Anna and Willard were very near the back of the books." Mary turned thirteen in January of 1878, and Laura turned eleven the next month. Carrie was going on eight.

Laura found many of her old friends at school, as well as Nellie and Willie Owens. There were also many newcomers sitting in the seats of the schoolhouse, including the Moses children, the Masters children and others. Laura swiftly got acquainted with them all, because she eagerly joined the games played before school and at recess. The classmates had snowball fights and races and were so rowdy that Mary was horrified.

Mary had always tried to control what she thought was Laura's wild behavior at recess. One day, as Laura was rushing out to join a snowball fight, Mary grabbed hold of her sister's long, brown hair and held her. "You're not going out!" she said. "I won't have it." Laura simply dragged Mary to the schoolhouse door, where they were both hit by the flying snowballs. Finally, Laura worked loose and ran into the cold outdoors, scooping up snow for the battle.

Although Laura was a tomboy and loved activity, she was also a keen student. Every Friday, there was a spell-down in school, and Laura could sometimes outspell the whole class. Spelling became so popular in Walnut Grove that winter that on Friday nights nearly the whole town assembled in the lamplit schoolhouse for spelling matches.

When spring came, Pa bought a lot in the big pasture behind Mr. Masters' hotel. Then Pa built a little house to live in, and when it was done, the family settled into their own home. It was restful and quiet to be alone once more, just Pa and Ma and Mary, Laura, Carrie and Grace. In the evenings, Pa played the fiddle again, and he even showed the girls how to dance. Mary and Laura became so practiced that sometimes when company came, they were asked to perform.

Pa always worked hard and could do almost any job well. He decided that Walnut Grove needed a butcher shop, so he opened one in the spring of 1878. People wanted fresh meat, and Pa did a good business. He was still in demand as a carpenter, and frequently left his shop to work at constructing or repairing buildings.

Ma felt comfortable and content in her own home once more. She never again wanted to live in a noisy hotel, or with another family, no matter how kind they were. She liked going to church in Walnut Grove, attending prayer meetings and helping the church ladies with projects. Although the Ingalls family was no longer farming, Ma was pleased that at least they were staying in one place.

The Walnut Grove school ran right through the spring and summer of 1878. The teacher was Sam Masters, the brother of the hotelkeeper. Pa bought Laura and Mary a new schoolbook for 61 cents; it was a history of the United States. Laura enjoyed studying history, and she was proud when Pa told her that some of his ancestors had come to Plymouth Colony on the *Mayflower*.

Laura had always considered Nellie Owens the most wretched girl in school, but someone new outdid the storekeeper's daughter in meanness and nasty manners. She was the teacher's daughter, Genevieve Masters. Genevieve considered herself far superior to the other students, because she wore fancier clothes and came from New York State. She sneered at the other children and lisped and sniveled in a way that Laura found maddening. Pa told Laura not to mind. He said there was nothing special about coming from New York; he had come from there himself.

Nellie and Genevieve became strong rivals.

Each girl wanted to control the leadership of all the girls. Laura was so independent that she would join neither group, despite Genevieve's wheedling and Nellie's gifts from her father's store. "Then to my surprise," Laura said, "I found myself leader of them all!"

Boys liked Laura too, and they invited her to join them playing ante-over, pullaway, prisoner's base and handball. When everyone saw how quick Laura was, she was invited to play in the baseball games for the rest of the school term. There was only one boy who could run faster than Laura Ingalls.

When school ended, Laura found a job. Mrs. Masters asked Ma if Laura could help out at the hotel washing dishes, waiting on tables and watching her son Will's baby. Laura would earn 50 cents a week, and Mrs. Masters promised she would not let her work too hard. When Laura started her job, she found it great fun. Like the hotel in Burr Oak, the one in Walnut Grove was full of interesting people and happenings. But at the end of the day, Laura could walk out the door and return to her own quiet home across the pasture.

Laura washed dishes, swept and dusted and

made beds in the hotel. She was too shy to enjoy waiting on tables full of hungry strangers, but she liked placing the dishes on the tables when the dining room was still and empty. During the quiet times between meals, Mrs. Masters let Laura disappear into a corner to read. She read through a stack of the *New York Ledger*, lost in the stories of the beautiful ladies, dashing men, dwarfs, secret caves and treacherous villains.

Laura's memory and her love of studying helped her win a prize at church. Every Sunday, the Ingalls family attended the Congregational church and Sunday School together, but in the afternoons, Laura went to the Methodist services as well. The Methodists were offering a prize to the child who could repeat from memory, without a mistake, the Golden Texts and Central Truths from the Bible. There were 104 Bible verses to remember. Week after week, Sunday School pupils tried and failed to recite the verses. Finally, only Laura and Howard Ensign were left. Both of them were perfect! There was only one prize Bible, but the minister's wife quietly told Laura that if she would wait awhile, a fancier edition would be sent for. Laura was content to wait.

People in Walnut Grove started noticing what a good worker Laura Ingalls was, and how careful she was in finishing a job. She was often asked to run errands for neighbors or to look after their babies. The nickels and dimes Laura was given were welcome, because Pa's wages were not much, and there was very little spare money in the Ingalls house. Even so, home was happy, and Laura did not want to leave when Mrs. Masters asked her to stay with a sick relative two miles out in the country. But when Laura thought of the money she could earn, she decided to go.

Sadie Hurley, Mrs. Masters' relative, was kind to Laura, but the days were long and lonely on the quiet prairie. Laura knew that her family back in Walnut Grove was in need of money, and Pa was restless about going west again. One night while she said her prayers, Laura felt so homesick and concerned about Pa and Ma and her sisters, she felt like crying. Then she thought over all those Bible verses she had memorized, and felt what she said was a "hovering, Presence, a Power comforting and sustaining me." Surprised, she thought, "This is what men call God." That experience helped Laura until she returned home. All through her life, Laura quietly relied on the belief that God would help her though difficulty.

Laura had just turned twelve years old during the winter of 1879 when Mary suddenly became sick. Mary felt a terrible pain in her head and had a fever so high that Ma cut off Mary's beautiful long hair to keep her cooler. Dr. Hoyt tended to Mary, but she grew so desperately ill that everyone thought she would die. Pa telegraphed for Dr. Wellcome from the distant town of Sleepy Eye, and he came on the train to help Mary.

"Brain fever" was what the doctors called Mary's illness. On the frontier, that could mean many kinds of ailments. The worst result of Mary's illness was that her eyesight grew dimmer as she recovered. She sat propped up on pillows, seeing less and less each day. The doctors shook their heads and could do nothing. They said nerves of Mary's eyes were dying. The last thing that she saw was the blue of Grace's eyes as she stood beside the chair where Mary sat.

On the sorrowful day when Mary could see no more, Pa solemnly gave Laura a duty. She must become Mary's link to light and color and action by describing what she saw of the world. Laura immediately started seeing twice, once for herself and again for her sister. This became Laura's lifelong habit.

Throughout her illness, Mary had not complained. When she became blind, Mary did not mourn. She was patient and accepting, and thankful for Pa and Ma and her sisters. Laura learned much from Mary. She practiced patience and cheerfulness and kindness, inspired by Mary's example. Laura was growing up.

During the days following Mary's illness, it seemed that the people of Walnut Grove talked of little else than the building of the railroads west into Dakota Territory. The railroad tracks ended in the town of Tracy, seven miles west of Walnut Grove. But there were rumors that the railroad line would be extended far into Dakota Territory to the west.

Railroads were important to the development of the frontier. They offered work to men at $1 a day while the tracks were being constructed. They lured Easterners to settle in the West. Towns sprang up along the tracks, and the freight trains brought goods and people into raw Western territories. For the farmer, the trains were a way to send crops back to Eastern markets from their Western homesteads.

Pa wanted to go west again, and he wanted to farm. But he had no money to start over. The hard years of the 1870's had left Pa in debt and with no savings. He saw no way to pay for tools and buildings and livestock, even if he could claim free homestead land. Finally, the railroad offered Pa a way to earn the money he needed.

One day not long after Mary's sight faded, she heard the sounds of a horse and buggy driving up to the little house in the Masters' pasture. The woman who came to the door was a stranger to Laura, but Pa and Ma knew her immediately. She was Pa's sister Docia, from Wisconsin. Her husband, Hi Forbes, was a contractor working for the railroad as it inched its way west. Docia stopped both to visit and to offer Pa a job. Each railroad camp had a company store, which sold goods to the workers. A store manager was needed to record purchases and keep track of the hours the men worked.

Pa immediately was anxious to accept the job his sister offered. It meant that he could work for good wages and hunt for some of Uncle Sam's free homestead land out in Dakota. Ma agreed to the plan, but reluctantly. She could think of many reasons to stay in Walnut Grove. She wondered about Mary: how would her blind daughter fare if they lived again on the frontier? Finally, Ma got the promise she wanted from Pa: when they settled in Dakota Territory, they would move no more. Their journeys would be ended.

Pa had to go west quickly with Docia, to begin his new job. He sold the house in Mr. Masters' pasture but arranged that Ma and the girls could stay there until Mary was stronger. The family would join Pa at the end of the summer.

Docia and Pa drove off together, bound for the railroad camps. Laura was now Ma's greatest help. Together they ran the house all summer and prepared for the move west. Daily, Laura took Mary for walks on the sunny prairie around Walnut Grove. Remembering her promise to Pa, Laura told Mary about everything she saw.

Letters came from Pa, with money from his paychecks. Finally a letter told Ma that he would meet the family at Tracy, where the railroad ended. Ma bought tickets and made the final preparations to leave Walnut Grove. This would be the girls' first train ride.

On the sunny September day when the Ingalls family left Walnut Grove, Laura looked through the train windows at the familiar sights. The buildings of Walnut Grove rushed past. The grasslands and plowlands and scattered farms on the prairie flashed by. The smoking engine speeded the train west. Once again, the Ingalls family was going into the unknown, in search of a new home.

7. Dakota Territory

P a met Ma and the girls at Tracy, and by wagon they continued west to the railroad camp near the Big Sioux River in Dakota Territory. Pa had been there all summer, keeping careful records of the hours the railroad employees worked. He also sold them goods from the store operated by the railroad company. The camp was miles away from any settlement, so the men had to buy what they needed from the company store. Each day, Pa kept a neat ledger of purchases, and the amounts were charged against the men's wages.

Looking over Pa's ledger, Laura read some of the purchases of June 1879:

1 pr. overalls	$1.00
1 shirt	.70
1 pr. boots	$4.40
1 pr. suspenders	.35

1 bushel corn	.52
1 loaf bread	.10
1 sack flour	$3.10
20 pounds nails	.80
2 pans	.35

The railroad men slept and ate in hastily built shanties constructed and operated by the company. For a month's food and shelter, $4.80 was deducted from a man's pay.

Pa brought his family to the Big Sioux railroad camp, but the work of preparing the railroad tracks there was nearly complete. The equipment and rough wooden shanties were being dismantled and moved farther west. After Pa's ledgers and accounts were checked for accuracy, he moved his family west with the construction crews, too.

Surveyors came to measure and map out a town where the railroad camp had been. This became the town of Brookings. Seven miles west, the town of Volga was established.

Laura loved being on the wide, empty Dakota prairie. To her, it was a friendly, never-ending meadow, stretching as far as she could see. The tall prairie grass waved in the wind, and white clouds sailed in the blue sky overhead. Cloud shadows moved across the green land. Old buffalo paths were etched in the ground, and circular depressions were scooped into the prairie where the buffalo had grazed. Pa said that these places were called buffalo wallows. But the buffalo were gone now, driven farther west. Laura was glad that she had seen their old grazing grounds before settlers and towns and railroads crowded in.

On the trip from the Big Sioux camp to the one farther west, Laura described the prairie to Mary. It was a long journey by wagon, nearly forty miles. The Ingalls family passed little sparkling lakes and wet, marshy sloughs, where rank grass grew as tall as six feet high. Prairie swells alternated with long flat stretches of level land. As the wagon rolled west, Laura felt a deep contentment. It was the same way Pa felt. The family was alone but safe, with only the wind and earth and sky and calling birds. Pa and Laura knew that sometime they must stop, but as they drove on, all the prairie seemed to belong to them.

When the sun sank, Laura was thrilled with the spectacle, and described it to Mary. "A ball of pulsing, liquid light, it sank in clouds of crimson and silver," she said. When the sun was gone, the prairie wind quieted and seemed to whisper mysteriously through the waving grass. Finally, far ahead, a few twinkling lights shone through the black night. It was the new railroad camp.

The railroad camp was built on the edge of a prairie lake. Some said later that Ma gave the lake its name. Looking at the water with the shining moonlight glimmering on its surface, Ma called it "Silver Lake."

The Ingalls family moved into a little shanty set apart from the bunkhouses, the company store and the cookhouse. Ma was firm when she told the girls that they must "keep to themselves." A railroad construction crew was not Ma's idea of good neighbors. So Pa worked daily with the men in the company store, while the girls stayed with Ma in the shanty. "Our interest centered all at home," Laura said.

There were very few women in the camp. One Irish family was there while the father worked on the railroad. Ma heard that their baby was sick, so she went to help, and her skill cured the child. The family wanted to pay her, but Ma would accept no money. Finally, the baby's father came to thank Ma again, blessing her with the name of every saint he knew. He quickly pressed a five-dollar gold piece into Ma's hand.

As the autumn days progressed, the railroad construction just north of the Silver Lake camp neared completion. The men and their teams and their plows and earth scrapers worked in a system that leveled uneven prairie, filling the low spots of ground and building embankments where the tracks would be laid. As the work ended, the men started leaving camp and heading back east for the winter.

In the spring, the tracks would be placed and a new town established alongside them. Pa learned that the town would be called De Smet in honor of a Catholic priest from Belgium, Father Pierre Jean De Smet. Father De Smet had been a missionary to the Sioux Indians and had been much loved by them. The Indians called him "Blackrobes."

As winter neared and Pa finished his accounting work for the railroad, he and Ma talked of returning east until spring. But one of the railroad surveyors asked Pa a favor. He wanted Pa to stay at the abandoned Silver Lake camp over the winter to guard the tools and railroad property being left there. The surveyor offered Pa a salary and the use of the house, which had been headquarters for the surveying team. It was well stocked with food and coal. On the treeless prairie, coal was a necessity for winter fuel.

The prairie was truly deserted when the railroad camp shut down on December 1, 1879. The surveyors left, the wild birds that had once screeched over Silver Lake were safe in the south and the two hundred construction workers were gone. Laura said that "we were left with only the abandoned shanties and the wind."

When the family moved into the Surveyors' House, they were snug for the winter. It was a well-built house, and in her book *By the Shores of Silver Lake*, Laura described it as large. There was a wide kitchen-dining-living room, a bedroom for Pa, Ma and Grace and a pantry and lean-to. Upstairs, the attic was a bedroom for Mary, Laura and Carrie. The lean-to held the coal, and the pantry was crammed with food. "It was all very comfortable and cozy," Laura said.

During the short winter days, Ma and the girls knitted, sewed, told stories and played games. Pa was often away, wandering over the empty prairie, hunting, trapping and looking over the country. In the evenings, after good meals prepared from the pantry's bounty, Pa again played the fiddle. Before winter set in, he had bought new books, magazines and newspapers. These were read by the light of the kerosene lamp that glowed over the red-checked tablecloth. Now the Ingalls family always read aloud, so that Mary could enjoy the stories.

When Pa hunted and tramped over the prairie, he looked over open land, searching for a homestead. One day he joyfully brought the news to Ma and the girls that he had found a perfect place, 160 acres of fine land just a mile from the townsite of De Smet. It was close enough to town for the girls to go to school easily.

At Christmastime, a young couple from Iowa came to Silver Lake. Robert and Ellie Boast surprised the Ingalls with their arrival. "I think it was the coldest night during the winter," Pa wrote, when "someone called out at the door. Upon going to the door, what was my surprise to see a woman on horseback, but upon looking a second time I saw a man also!"

The Boasts settled into one of the abandoned railroad shanties, and they were jolly company for the rest of the winter. They had come early, to establish their homestead claim in the spring. The Boasts told Pa that so many people were coming to Dakota when winter broke that there would be a land rush.

Pa had seen evidence of the coming throng of land seekers. On his hunting trips, he saw rough shanties built on the prairie and other signs of civilization. One day he came home, telling the girls that just two miles north of Silver Lake he had explored two empty claim shanties. In one, old clothes hung on a nail. Inside a pocket was an envelope addressed to someone named "Almanzo Wilder." In the other shanty the name "Royal Wilder" was written on a big card and left on a rough plank bunk.

In February 1880, not long after Laura's thirteenth birthday, Pa drove off for Brookings, where a government land office had been established. There he filed a claim to the homestead he had found near De Smet. He discovered many other newcomers at the office, eagerly filing on quarter sections (160 acres was a quarter of a square mile) of the free land. Settlers could pay the government $1.25 per acre for a 160-acre tract, or they could homestead. Pa told the girls that homesteading was a bet with

Uncle Sam to see if a man could stay on the land for the five-year requirement.

Early in the spring of 1880, land seekers started arriving on the prairie. Because the Surveyors' House was the only building for miles around, Pa and Ma found themselves unexpectedly in the hotel business again. Strangers who came to the door were hungry and cold. They were glad to pay Ma 25 cents for a meal and another 25 cents to sleep in their blankets on the floor around the stove.

Ma and Laura worked hard feeding the new-comers. They fried salt pork and potatoes, made baked beans and brewed hot tea, and Ma baked her delicious sourdough biscuits. There was no milk available, so her bread and biscuits were made from dough using soured water and flour. When a visitor asked Ma for some of her recipes, she found it hard to explain how much of each ingredient she used. "Goodness!" she exclaimed. "I never measure anything!"

The Surveyors' House became as hectic and noisy as the hotel in Burr Oak had been, but Laura was happy to see the money mount up from the meals and sleeping places they sold. She knew that it would be expensive to start a new farm on the prairie in the spring.

The Ingalls family was surprised and happy to see the Reverend Edward Alden from Walnut Grove among a crowd of men who wanted to spend the night. He was being sent west again to start new Congregational churches along the railroad line. The first church service in De Smet was held in the Surveyors' House. Mr. and Mrs. Boast and the Ingalls family were the congregation. Ma knew that history was being made, so she wrote down the date of that first service: February 29, 1880.

On the first of March, Laura and Carrie walked from the Surveyors' House to the townsite of De Smet nearby. There was very little to see. Carrie came home complaining that all she saw were sticks stuck in the ground. Ma explained that those were stakes to indicate lots where houses, stores, a church and a school would be.

Pa bought lots along what would become De Smet's Main Street. He tore down abandoned railroad shanties for lumber and built two store buildings. One of them he sold, and the other he kept as an investment. Then a man named Harthorne also built a store, and a Mr. Beardsley constructed a hotel. Lumber was hard to obtain on the prairie and had to be hauled from the east by wagon until trains started arriving regularly at the new townsite.

"Those were great days," Laura said of the building of De Smet in April 1880. Sixteen buildings were quickly erected. A newspaper called *The Kingsbury County News* was started. The county was organized, and Pa was called in to help as the first settler of the townsite. He was elected Justice of the Peace.

It was an exciting day when the railroad track was finally completed, and trains started regularly arriving and departing from De Smet. Homesteaders flooded in from the East, among them the Wilder brothers and their sister, Eliza Jane, from Spring Valley, Minnesota. The surveyors returned, and the Ingalls family then moved into Pa's store on Main Street.

"In those days," Laura observed, "once people started going west, they usually kept on going, making stops along the way." It did not surprise the Ingalls family to meet again in De Smet some of the old friends they had known in the Big Woods and in Walnut Grove. George and Maggie Masters arrived in De Smet from Walnut Grove, and Ma invited them to stay in the store. While they were there, their son was born, the first baby born in De Smet.

Despite the excitement of the building of the town around her, Laura knew that it was the end of the old free days of the prairie.

Town life was not what the Ingalls family wanted. They were eager to begin farming again. As soon as he could, Pa built a shanty on the homestead claim. It was a tiny house, so small that Ma could only laugh when she saw it. "It looks like half a woodshed that has been split along the ridgepole." The shanty was covered with black tar paper when the family moved their belongings out to the homestead.

There was much to do at the homestead. A well had to be dug, shelter for the horses and livestock had to be built. Pa's plow began to cut into the tough prairie sod as he worked long days turning up the soil. A garden was planted. Although De Smet was just a mile away, Laura did not go there all summer. She was busy helping Pa and working with Ma in the shanty and in the garden.

All over the green prairie, families like the Ingallses were starting homes.

Laura wished, as Pa did, that they could go still farther west. But her journeys were limited to walks with Mary to the low hill on the homestead. Often they went at sunset time, when the air was luminous and Mary could feel the light on her face. As the sun dropped in the sky and clouds were tinted with purple and gold and pink and red, Laura described the prairie spectacle.

"You make pictures when you talk, Laura," Mary would say.

Laura was thrilled to witness those western sunsets. But she hoped one day to see what was beyond Dakota Territory, where the Ingalls family had safely settled on their homestead.

8. Prairie Girl

The first summer and autumn on the homestead came to an abrupt end when a fierce blizzard swept over Dakota Territory on October 15, 1880. For three days, blowing snow filled the air, and Laura said, "The wind shrieked and howled like nothing under heaven but a blizzard wind." The intensity of this early storm stunned many of the new settlers. Pa was concerned; he knew how thin-walled the shanty on the claim was.

An old Sioux Indian wandered into De Smet one autumn day with a solemn pronouncement. He said that a terrible winter was ahead. On the prairie, the Sioux Indians expected severe winters every seventh year; 1880 ended a third seven-year cycle, and the Indians predicted the cold and snow would be especially severe.

The Indian's prophecy convinced Pa that he should move his family to town. His building at the corner of Main and Second Street stood solid and empty and would be a good place to spend the winter. Pa hauled his haystacks there, and one day he and Ma loaded the wagon with furniture, clothes and bedding. They settled in town in time for Laura and Carrie to begin school.

De Smet had grown during its first year. A Congregational Church had been started, and the school building was ready to open. Laura and Carrie joined the fifteen pupils of De Smet's first school, which opened the first of November.

Another unexpected blizzard struck during a school day, and Laura and Carrie struggled to find their way home. Blizzards always interrupted activity in a western town like De Smet. The little settlements were all dependent on the daily trains for food supplies, fuel and mail delivery. When snow blocked the tracks and drifts filled the railroad cuts that had been hollowed through the hills, trains were delayed.

Pa and other men from De Smet helped clean off the railroad tracks with shovels, but as quickly as they finished the job, a new blizzard seemed to strike. It was not long until coal supplies were low, and stores started to run out of food. School was canceled indefinitely until there was coal to heat the building.

The blizzards continued. Christmas came and went without a train. In the narrow kitchen of Pa's building, the Ingalls family crowded together around the stove. Laura tried to continue studying her schoolbooks and repeated all the lessons to Mary, but it was hard to read in the dim light. The windows were gray sheets of swirling snow. Ma lit the lamp only when she had to, in order to conserve the precious kerosene.

The small stocks of food in De Smet began to give out. Laura and Ma gasped when Pa reported that the last sack of flour in town sold for $50, and the last sugar for $1 a pound. Without coal, some people carelessly burned lumber, purchased at high prices. But Pa was thrifty and had better ideas. He told the family they would keep warm with hay.

Using the hay he had hauled from the home-stead, Pa and Laura twisted hay into sticks. "A handful of hay," Laura explained, "was twisted into a rope, then doubled and allowed to twist back on itself, and the two ends came together in a knot."

Through the long winter, those hay sticks fed the hungry stove, keeping the temperature in the kitchen above freezing.

In January 1881, the railroad company announced that it was suspending service until spring. It could not cope with blizzards that struck frequently and that often lasted for days, with snowdrifts that sometimes reached forty feet.

For the Ingalls family, what became known as the "Hard Winter" was a daily battle for heat and food. Most people were too petrified to leave shelter during the short breaks between blizzards. Only Pa and the two Wilder brothers ventured out of De Smet to haul in loads of hay.

Royal and Almanzo Wilder spent the Hard Winter in their grain and feed store on Main Street. On their homesteads north of town, they had raised wheat crops and cut stacks of hay during the previous summer. The brothers sold hay in De Smet; their supply of wheat was a secret. Only Pa knew that it was hidden in the feed store. The Wilders wanted to plant their seed wheat in the spring, not sell it to the hungry people in De Smet. No one knew if the railroads would ship seed wheat in time for spring planting.

When the Ingalls food supplies were nearly gone and the stores had nothing to sell, the Wilders secretly sold Pa a sack of their precious wheat. The wheat was ground into flour with a coffee mill and Ma baked brown bread or biscuits for her family's skimpy meals.

Laura turned fourteen during the Hard Winter. She stoutly helped Pa and Ma weather the storms and helped cheer Mary, Carrie and Grace. She led them in singing songs they knew from Sunday School, and songs they had sung for as long as she remembered. They memorized Bible verses and pieces from *The Independent Fifth Reader*. And in the dim light of the kitchen, Laura started writing poetry. One of her Hard Winter poems showed humor in the face of the terrible weather:

> We remember not the summer
> For it was long ago
> We remember not the summer
> In this whirling blinding snow
> I will leave this frozen region
> I will travel farther south
> If you say one word against it
> I will hit you in the mouth.

As the winter dragged on, Almanzo Wilder and

one of Laura's classmates, Cap Garland, made a daring trip across the prairie to find a supply of wheat to bring back to De Smet. The town was so close to famine that only this desperate search could help. The boys found a settler with wheat, bought it, and hauled it to town, arriving just before another blizzard hit.

The weeks and months slowly passed by with little relief from the blizzard winds and snow. Not until April did the storms finally stop. And not until May 10 did the first train arrive in De Smet. The whole winter's worth of ice and snow packed down on the tracks had taken weeks to melt and clear away.

"There is something about living close to the great elemental forces of nature that allows people to rise above small annoyances and discomforts," Laura observed after the winter was over. Everyone in De Smet had survived, but the new settlers had to admit that on the Dakota prairie, nature's strength must be respected.

As soon as the snow melted, the Ingalls family left town and returned to their homestead claim. Pa added two rooms to the shanty and worked long hours behind his plow, enlarging the fields and planting crops of wheat and corn. Mary and Laura took their walks again and talked of plans for Mary's education.

The Reverend Alden had told Pa and Ma about the Iowa College for the Blind in the town of Vinton. A relative of his was a teacher there. The school helped blind students learn to be independent and offered a high school and college course of studies. As soon as they heard of the school, the Ingalls family hoped to send Mary there. During the summer of 1881, they made preparations for her enrollment. Mary had always loved learning; she had always hoped to be a teacher. The school for the blind was a wonderful opportunity for Mary.

Laura was so eager to help earn money for Mary's school clothes that she took a job in De Smet, sewing at a dry goods store. Pa often walked with her to town in the mornings. He was working on most of the new buildings springing up in De Smet.

Working in the cramped, hot store on Main Street, Laura realized how much she loved the country, and how lucky her family was on their homestead. The 25 cents Laura earned each day added up to $9 for Mary by summer's end, but

Laura also bought some treats for herself. She purchased a plume for her bonnet for 60 cents, a thimble for 10 cents, a pair of cloth shoes for $1 and four yards of calico for 36 cents.

In the fall, Pa and Ma took Mary to Vinton to enroll in school. They traveled by train and were excited to reach the big brick school building on Asylum Street, with its walkways where the students could exercise and the farm that bordered the campus. The teachers all made Mary welcome, and Pa and Ma were impressed with the studies offered by the school.

Mary was sixteen when she started at the Iowa College for the Blind. Laura helped her learn so thoroughly after she became blind that Mary was well prepared for the academic course work. She studied natural history, chemistry, algebra, political economy, physiology and rhetoric. She excelled at music, learning to play the piano and organ. Patiently, Mary learned what was called "Fancy Work" and mastered sewing, knitting, weaving and beadwork. She learned to make hammocks, and fly nets for horses.

The family in De Smet was lonesome for Mary but happy that she had resumed her education. As

Laura said, "I wanted an education so much myself that I was very happy in thinking that Mary was getting one." Laura planned to prepare herself for teaching; it was a tradition in Ma's family. And Laura wanted very much to help to earn money for Mary's school expenses, as well as for her own clothes and needs. She knew Pa was investing what he could in developing their farm. Money was scarce.

During the winters following the Hard Winter, the Ingalls family returned to De Smet each fall, to live in Pa's building. Laura was very concerned with her schoolwork, because she wanted to earn a teacher's certificate when she was sixteen. Although she and Carrie were at first shy among the new students at school, they quickly made friends and settled into the routine of lessons and studying, with homework around the lamp at home at night.

Laura enjoyed her friendship with girls such as Mary Power, Minnie Johnson and Ida Brown, the new Congregational minister's adopted daughter. But she was horrified one day to see a new girl enter the schoolroom, an unpleasant reminder of Walnut Grove. She was Genevieve Masters. The Masters family had moved to De Smet, and Genevieve was more snobbish and mean-spirited to Laura than she had ever been.

Miss Eliza Jane Wilder was the schoolteacher during the fall of 1882. The "lady homesteader" had settled on a claim near her brothers Royal and Almanzo. Pa was on the school board, and its members had begged Miss Wilder to teach the De Smet school.

While Miss Wilder was in charge, the school was in an uproar of disobedience and noise. Laura worried that her studies would be so interrupted that she could not earn a teacher's certificate. Genevieve Masters, Laura said, was "the last unbearable straw." She began creating trouble between Laura and her friends. Then she told untrue tales about Laura to Miss Wilder, who believed them. Laura was so annoyed with Miss Wilder that she despaired in rhyme, writing:

> I feel like a borned fool
> For coming to this blamed school
> What is the use of coming here?
> Where there is no one to love or fear.

Laura's friend Mary Power shared Laura's attitude about Miss Wilder's teaching. She wrote:

> By gum I must leave the school
> For teacher looks like such a fool.

Fortunately Miss Wilder taught only during the fall term of 1882. She was followed by Mr. Clewett, Mr. Seeley and finally Professor Owen. Laura was a leader in her class, and teachers expected and got her best work. She was especially talented at history and writing. In the evenings after she had finished studying, Laura often made rhymes and wrote long verses. She wrote so many poems that she created little books and penned in the verses in her neat handwriting. On the cover of one of her books she wrote:

> When you open this book
> Just take one good look
> If the rhymes do not please
> You can close it with ease.

And on the back she wrote:

> If you've read this book through
> With all its jingles
> I'll let you know that it's been filled,
> By Laura E. Ingalls

During summers on the homestead claim, Laura still spent hours with her books. Good reports were coming from the College for the Blind about Mary's progress, and Laura felt she must do her share to keep her sister there. That meant keeping up on her studies, in preparation for becoming a teacher.

One of Laura's poems expressed the way she felt about hard work and achievement:

> If you've anything to do
> Do it with all your might
> Don't let trifles hinder you
> If you're sure you're right
> Work away
> Do it with all your might.

9. Teaching, Courtship and Marriage

In December of 1882, Laura Ingalls recited half the story of American history at a school exhibition in De Smet. Ida Brown recited the other half. Since Laura and Ida were among the oldest and best students, they had been assigned this role in the evening performance of recitations, oral readings and demonstrations of learning. Laura was nervous and always a trifle bashful in crowds, but the applause was thunderous when she finished her part of the program.

Many people were impressed by Laura's performance in the school exhibition, including the

Ingallses' good friends from Silver Lake, Robert and Ellie Boast. One day just before Christmas, Mr. Boast and his cousin Mr. Bouchie visited at the Ingallses' home.

To Laura's surprise, they had stopped to see not Pa, but her! Laura was even more amazed to learn that Mr. Bouchie was a school board member from a little settlement twelve miles south of De Smet. And his school district wanted Laura to teach a two-month winter term for them!

Laura's sixteenth birthday was not until February, and she knew that sixteen was the legal age for a beginning teacher. Mr. Bouchie simply told Laura not to mention that fact; if she would agree to teach at the Bouchie School, he would arrange with the county superintendent to examine her immediately. Teachers were hard to find and Mr. Bouchie wanted Laura for his school. By the end of the day, Laura held in her hand both a teaching certificate and a contract to teach the Bouchie School at $20 a month during January and February—about twice as much as her mother had earned twenty-six years earlier.

Laura had to live with Mr. and Mrs. Bouchie

and their young son while she taught. Mrs. Bouchie was unfriendly to Laura and, like some prairie women, depressed by the isolation and ceaseless winds blowing over the empty land. Laura was anxious to leave their claim shanty each morning to report to the schoolhouse, which was an abandoned homesteader's shanty a half mile away.

Her students numbered only five. Laura sometimes felt she was failing in her work of teaching her first school, but she plodded through the days. She patterned school days after classes in De Smet, and studied her own lessons while her pupils learned theirs.

Laura felt so unwelcome at the Bouchie house that she dreaded spending a weekend with her miserable hosts. Secretly she hoped Pa would come out to take her home, but twelve miles was a long journey in the winter. As her first week of teaching ended, Laura was astonished to hear sleigh bells ringing outside the schoolhouse. She was even more amazed to see that behind a team of brown Morgan horses, wrapped in a buffalo-skin coat, was Almanzo Wilder.

Laura was confused at Almanzo's offer to take her home and return her to the Bouchie household on Sunday. It was almost too cold to speak on the ride home, and Laura was tongue-tied and bashful as well, considering herself poor company.

All through the eight weeks at Bouchie School, Almanzo took Laura back and forth on the weekends, patiently and silently braving temperatures often below zero. "Much as I longed to go home for those two days, I did not want to be unfair or deceitful," Laura recalled. Once she told Almanzo bluntly that when school was out, she would no longer ride with him. But he continued to fetch her on Fridays.

After the homesick weeks of teaching were finished, Laura was proud to receive her pay, which she gave to Pa. She had done a fine job at the Bouchie School. Her students had learned from her and respected her. Laura knew that she could find another teaching job easily. But she would not go so far in the winter again.

Back in De Smet, Laura returned to school. Her teacher, Professor Ven Owen, always demanded the best his students could produce. He was convinced that Laura Ingalls was his most promising student, and told Pa that she "had a wonderful mind and should be given every opportunity for an education." Professor Owen especially stressed writing skills with his classes, requiring them to compose essays about what they thought and read. Laura's compositions were always exceptional, so well done that Professor Owen used her work as examples to show the whole school. He was very proud of her.

Though she had taught, Laura was still a school-girl and liked the same fun and pastimes that her friends Minnie and Mary and Ida did. When a skating rink opened in De Smet, Laura could not resist skipping school to spend an afternoon there, and she was surprised to see that many of her classmates had the same idea. The next day, Professor Owen solemnly questioned his students about their whereabouts, and all had to answer that they had been "at the rink." Professor Owen told Laura he expected her to be a good example to her class and spoke so sincerely that she decided never to miss school again if she could avoid it.

De Smet had grown quickly since 1880, and there were many activities during the winters when the Ingalls family lived in town. They were involved in the Congregational Church and Sunday School. There were church suppers and socials and Christmas-tree celebrations to attend. A literary society was started and almost everyone in town went to the Friday night meetings. Laura was asked to parties by Ernie Perry and Lawyer Thomas, but admitted much later that she secretly admired Cap Garland and Fred Gilbert, who were already courting her girlfriends. Laura and her friends all thought a young Swedish boy named Oscar Rhuel was a romantic figure. He worked as a hired man for the Wilder brothers, Royal and Almanzo.

Almanzo seemed to have forgotten Laura's telling him she would not ride with him after she'd finished at the Bouchie School. He continued to appear at Pa's door with his fine Morgan horses, asking Laura for sleigh rides. In the spring, when the Ingalls family moved back to the homestead, Almanzo arrived there with a shiny black buggy.

On their rides over the prairie, Laura learned about Almanzo. He was ten years older than she was and was a homesteader with 320 acres of land. His family lived in Spring Valley, Minnesota, but before that, the Wilders had farmed in Malone, New York. There Almanzo had developed his love for Morgan horses, which Laura shared. He had worked hard for his Morgan team, and then he had saved for a driving buggy.

On one of their drives together, Laura and Almanzo discussed their names. Almanzo's parents called him "Manzo" and his brother Royal called him "Mannie." Laura said she thought both nicknames were ugly and silly. She told Almanzo that she would call him "Manly."

Manly said that his oldest sister was named Laura, and he had never liked the name, so he wanted a nickname for her, too. When Laura said that her middle name was Elizabeth, Manly decided to call her "Bessie."

During the spring of 1884, Laura taught her second school. It was called the Perry School and was just a short walk south of Pa's homestead land. Laura's pay was $25 a month for April, May and June, and she taught only three students. Laura said that "helping them with their lessons was a pleasure." While the children studied, Laura worked in her own schoolbooks. At the end of the day, she walked across the green springtime prairie to Pa's house on the claim.

Laura was so ambitious that she often worked on Saturdays for the dressmaker in De Smet. She sewed well and worked quickly, and was in much demand to help fill orders for new clothes the townspeople needed. Laura earned clothes for herself in this way, using her wages to buy materials and patterns and hats to wear to church and when Manly came courting. Pa had bought Ma a new sewing machine, and Ma marveled at its speed. For years she had stitched clothing for Pa, herself and the four girls by hand, and now she welcomed the convenience of using the new machine. The whir of the sewing machine filled the house on the homestead while Ma worked.

Another sound filled the house too. With Laura's salary from the Perry School and some money that Pa added, a pump organ was purchased for Mary. The family knew that Mary excelled in music lessons at the College for the Blind and wanted her to continue practicing at home on her summer vacations. Pa added a sitting room to the claim shanty to make room for the organ, and then the shanty could rightfully be called a house. The farm was prospering, and though Pa sometimes wished they could move west again, he realized that he and Ma were settled permanently in Dakota Territory.

Mary's summer vacations were exciting times for the Ingalls family. School trained her to function independently in the world, so Mary made the long railroad journeys from Vinton to De Smet alone. She talked happily of her friends at school, her studies, the literary society she belonged to, and the many crafts she had mastered. Her careful beadwork pieces—tiny beads strung on fine wire—were a marvel to Mary's family and friends. She brought home presents for everyone—watch cases, jewelry, bookmarks, vases and baskets—all created with the skill of her sensitive fingers.

Almanzo Wilder continued to come to Pa's house to visit Laura. During the week, Almanzo was busy working on his farm north of De Smet, but on Sundays he appeared with horses and buggy, asking Laura to go riding. Sometimes Pa and Ma disapproved of his horses; Almanzo once bought a frisky, untamed team named Skip and Barnum. Barnum, he told Laura, was named for P. T. Barnum, the famous circus showman. Laura had to dash to jump into the buggy, because the team could not be stopped for long. But she loved the fast horses that led her and Manly over the prairie. Laura and Manly drove to the twin lakes, Henry and Thompson, and to Spirit Lake, with its ancient Indian burial mounds. They raced through De Smet, and people stared. They sometimes drove across the prairie, covering sixty-five miles in an afternoon. Manly told Laura there was not another man in town who would try to drive Skip and Barnum. Laura remembered that "Pa said Manly was trying to kill me. But it was the most fun I ever had!"

"I kept going with Manly, and people began to take it seriously," Laura recalled. Although Laura was independent, she now did nothing to discourage Manly from his attentions. They went to De Smet's big Fourth of July celebration in 1884, with fireworks and races. They attended a singing school held at the Congregational church and went to dances and ice cream socials.

One night as Manly and Laura rode back to Pa's homestead, Manly asked Laura if she would like an engagement ring. She was seventeen and he was twenty-seven; they were old enough to marry and try homesteading on their own. Laura accepted a gold engagement ring from Manly, set with pearls and garnets. When she showed it to Ma, Ma said, "Pa and I haven't been blind. We've been expecting it." Pa just smiled when he saw the ring on Laura's finger.

When school started in the fall of 1884, it was in

a big, new, two-story building. De Smet had already outgrown its first school. Laura and Carrie were both in the high school room upstairs while seven-year-old Grace studied with the first-floor primary students. Pa had decided to sell his store on Main Street, and so he improved the house on the homestead, making it solid enough to keep the family snug in winter. They would live on the farm year round, and Pa promised to take the girls to school each day. He was often busy in town anyway, doing carpentry work or filing court cases as part of his job as Justice of the Peace. He also served as town clerk, deputy sheriff, street commissioner and a school board and church board member.

Not long after Laura started her last year of school, Manly and Royal Wilder left on a long trip. Royal had opened a variety store in De Smet, and he outfitted a peddler's wagon with goods to sell or trade. The brothers planned to go to the big fair called the New Orleans Exposition in Louisiana and then travel north again to visit their parents in Spring Valley, Minnesota. Laura did not expect to see Manly again until the springtime.

It was perhaps during the weeks when Manly

was away that Laura wrote poetry again, this time expressing how she felt as her fiancé traveled so far from Dakota. . . .

> Lonely! I am so lonely
> Far from thee.
> Days come and go,
> And are all the same
> To me.
> For thou, my beloved one
> No more I see
> No more I hear thy footstep
> Strong and free;
> Nor meet thee, neath the scarlet
> Maple tree.
> Oh my beloved one! wherever
> Thou mayest be,
> Wandering on a foreign shore
> Or on the sea,
> Come, I recall thee
> Home to me.

Manly surprised all the Ingalls family when he appeared at the door of the homestead house on Christmas Eve. He, too, was lonely for Laura. "I couldn't stay all winter," he explained, and then, as Laura said, "He kissed me before all the folks."

Laura wanted to teach school one more term, to help Pa and Ma one last time before she married. (Only single women could teach school.) In the spring of 1885, she agreed to teach the Wilkins School, north of De Smet. This meant that once more Laura would need to leave her own class before the term was over.

Professor Owen was troubled when Laura told him of her plans. His eyes filled with tears as he begged Laura to complete the school year. He had wanted Laura's class to graduate together, but knew that only she would pass the examinations. So he held the others back for another year. Professor Owen pleaded with Laura to give up teaching so that he could graduate her from high school by herself.

Laura felt she must keep her promise to teach the Wilkins School, but as she admitted, "This was a great unhappiness to me. I had always so longed for an education, and had hoped at least to graduate from high school."

But teaching the Wilkins School was a pleasure. Her pay was $30 a month for April, May and June. She lived with the Wilkins family, who were cheerful and pleasant. Her pupils learned quickly. And every Friday, Manly came riding over the prairie to take her home for the weekend. He was busy improving his land and building a house where they would live when they married.

When Laura's duties at the Wilkins School were over, there were long summer days to spend with Mary, who was home for vacation. Again they walked over Pa's homestead land, and experienced the sunsets together. Laura told her sister that next summer there would be two homes to visit; by then Laura would be settled on Manly's farm.

Laura and Manly had planned to be married when the fall harvest work was done, but they heard that bossy Eliza Jane Wilder wanted to plan a big wedding for them. Neither Laura nor Manly wanted Eliza Jane's help, so they decided to marry sooner than they had expected to.

Very quietly, on the morning of August 25, 1885, Laura and Almanzo drove to the Reverend Brown's house and were married. Laura had asked for a change in the wording of the wedding ceremony. She objected to the use of the word "obey." "Even if I tried, I do not think I could obey anyone against my better judgment," she explained. Both Reverend Brown and Manly agreed with her.

After their wedding, Mr. and Mrs. Almanzo Wilder drove back to Pa and Ma's for dinner. Then Manly and Laura said good-bye to Pa and Ma and Carrie and Grace. (Mary had returned to school in Vinton.) As they had so many times before, Laura and Manly rode across the prairie and through De Smet. Two miles north, they came to the little house Manly had built for them.

Laura Ingalls Wilder was no longer a pioneer girl. She was a homesteader's wife. And, she thought happily: "I had a house and home of my own."

10. "We Want to See the World!"

"I was a little awed at my new estate," Laura said of the farm home where she lived with Manly after their wedding. The Wilder land began a mile straight north of De Smet. Instead of the usual quarter section of 160 acres of homestead land, Manly had filed on two quarter sections. The second was a "tree claim" farther north. The government allowed settlers simultaneous second claims if they planted ten acres of the land with young trees. On Manly's tree claim the required acres of cottonwoods, elms and box elders were thriving when the building of the Wilders' first house was completed. One day the trees would shade and cool the little house.

Laura was pleased with the home her husband

had built. It was a neat little frame house, painted a soft gray. Windows in the living room, bedroom and kitchen let in the sunlight and views of the green prairie and the blue sky overhead. Laura quickly felt at home and was delighted when she discovered a wonderful cabinet in her pantry Almanzo had made himself. Drawers and cupboards were expertly fitted to provide Laura with space for every need. As a married woman, Laura knew she would now have to manage her housekeeping as skillfully as Ma always had.

After the wedding, Manly decided to put more of his land into cultivation immediately; with over three hundred acres, he could raise bountiful crops. He and Laura discussed plans for the farm together. Manly valued Laura's ideas, and they decided to approach wheat farming on the prairie as a team. Laura quickly found that her contribution was meager. When she sent eggs to town with Manly to trade, they brought just 5 cents a dozen, and no one wanted her butter at any price.

"It took money in quite some amount to get started on a farm there at that time," Laura remembered, when she thought over the first years the Wilders spent on the Dakota farm. There was expensive machinery to buy. Horses were needed to power the field machines, and horses needed plenty of feed as well as shelter. Sometimes men had to be hired to help Manly, especially at harvesttime. Though they disliked it, the Wilders' debts mounted. Even the little gray house was mortgaged for $500.

To save the cost of paying a hired man, Laura often helped Manly with the farm work. "I learned to do all kinds of farm work with machinery," she said. "I have ridden the binder, driving six horses." Though their work was hard, Manly and Laura believed that their acres of rich prairie land would one day produce for them lavishly. They had the hope and patience of the farmer and the belief that the next year would be better than the one before.

When their work was done, and on Sundays, Manly and Laura had happy times. They visited their friends in De Smet, or their friends drove out to the tree claim for meals and conversation. They attended concerts and church socials in town, and often visited Pa and Ma and the girls on the homestead.

One of Laura's favorite memories of her early married life was the horseback rides she and Manly shared. In their stable were two swift ponies, Trixy and Fly. Sometimes before breakfast, Manly and Laura would saddle the horses and ride off across the prairie. Laura learned to imitate a cowboy yell that set her Trixy off like a streak. Often Laura had to stop her horse while Manly and Fly caught up to them.

The Wilders took their usual long buggy rides together during the spring of 1886. On Sunday afternoons they rode far over the greening prairies. June was always Laura's favorite month on the prairie because it was the time when the wild roses bloomed. The low bushes of pink and red blossoms colored the land, and the sweet scent of flowers filled the warm air. Laura and Manly were expecting their first child, and the rose-covered land suggested a name to Laura.

As they wondered about names for their baby and Manly pointed out that they needed to wait and see if a boy or girl was born, Laura abruptly settled the matter. "It will be a girl and we will call her Rose," she said.

That summer of 1886 was a bumper season for more than wild roses. Crops grew lush and promising; Manly said he'd never seen such wheat. Laura estimated that their wheat crop would bring $3,000. They could pay their taxes, pay for their house, pay for the farm machinery and still be rich!

One hot August day, just before Manly planned to harvest the wheat, the sky darkened and great sweeps of hail pounded the land. From their house, the Wilders watched breathlessly as the storm increased. When it was over, they realized that their crop was gone. The grain was pounded into the wet ground. The wheat field was ruined.

With their baby due in December and expenses mounting, Laura and Manly knew they must reorganize their plans. They found that they could mortgage their homestead land to raise money to pay some of their bills. But the bank required that they live on the homestead land, which was a short distance from the tree claim. They improved the shanty on the homestead land, and on their first wedding anniversary, they closed the little gray house and moved. The shanty stood on the top of a long sloping hill. From its top Laura could see De Smet to the south, the Wessington Hills to the west, Spirit Lake to the north and Silver Lake to the east.

Manly improved the homestead during the fall and made plans for the next year's crops. Mostly

Laura sat quietly in her rocking chair, waiting for the birth of her baby.

Just as Laura had predicted, the baby was a girl. On the night of December 5, 1886, Rose Wilder was born. She was a healthy, big baby. Ma stayed a few days to help, and then a hired girl came to work for Laura for a while. But for most of the winter, Manly, Laura and Rose were alone in the cozy, isolated shanty on the prairie.

Laura and Manly's dreams of a strong crop in 1887 did not come true. Because of hot winds and dry weather, the crops were meager. That summer some of the hay crop and the barn burned in a mysterious fire. Laura worried, and sometimes wondered if they should give up farming. But Manly was more patient and believed they could be successful.

Pa and Ma had wearied of trying to farm their homestead. At Christmastime in 1887, they moved to De Smet permanently. Pa built a comfortable little house for the family on Third Street, not far from the church and close to the school Carrie and Grace attended. Pa still did most of the carpentry jobs in town. He and Ma lived in De Smet for the rest of their lives, and never moved again.

Little Rose was quickly whisked to Pa's house

during the winter of 1888. Laura and Manly contracted diphtheria and for weeks they lay sick while Rose was safe in town. Royal Wilder nursed Laura and Manly as best he could, but their recovery was slow.

Manly was most seriously affected, and partially paralyzed, by the illness. When he could leave his sickbed, he moved painfully. His feet were partially lame, and with great difficulty he shuffled and struggled to walk. Even his hands were affected. He had been a vigorous thirty-year-old man before the sickness came, and after it left, he worked constantly to regain his strength and his ability to run the farm.

Often Laura left her own work in the house to help Manly with some task his clumsy fingers could no longer do. He could drive the team with the plow, but he could no longer hitch up the horses. The 320 acres of land were too much for Manly to farm. A buyer purchased the homestead quarter, and the Wilders moved back to the tree claim and the little gray house.

With weather conditions so uncertain and the outcome of their crops so unpredictable, Laura and Manly talked of raising sheep on the farm. Laura's cousin Peter Ingalls had moved to De Smet. He offered to be the Wilders' partner, so together they bought a hundred Shropshire sheep. Peter lived with the Wilders and was a great help to Manly, who was still weak.

The growing season in 1889 was a dry one. Longingly Laura and Manly looked up at the sky, hoping to see signs of rain. The tree claim plantings struggled to survive, along with the garden and field crops. For weeks, the winds were so hot that they burned the wheat and oat crops until they died. "How I wish it would rain!" Laura's sister Grace mourned in her diary. And Laura spoke of "how heartbreaking it was, to watch the grain we had sown with such hope wither and yellow in the hot winds."

Although the weather had destroyed the crops, the Wilders still had something to look forward to. They expected a new baby in August. The baby was born on a hot afternoon, a boy. "He looked just like Manly," Grace Ingalls observed. But he did not live. On August 10, 1889, the De Smet newspaper reported that "Mr. and Mrs. A. J. Wilder's little child died Wednesday evening."

The Wilders' baby boy was buried in an unmarked grave in the De Smet cemetery. He had no name; Laura's feelings were so numbed and sorrowful that she hardly wanted anyone to mention her son to her. Rose was too young to remember her brother, but she did know that "my mother wanted nothing said about it; I think she never stopped grieving and it was her way to be silent about any unhappy subject."

Laura felt that she only wanted to rest after the baby's death. Rose was nearly three and could help with simple chores, including feeding the stove with haysticks. One afternoon Rose was fueling the stove when the hay in her arms caught fire. She dropped the burning hay, and almost immediately the kitchen was ablaze.

Laura could only scramble out of the burning house with Rose; she was too weak to fight the fire. By the time neighbors saw the flames and Manly rushed in from the fields, the house was burning uncontrollably. Only a few things were saved: Laura's wedding silver, and some clothes and dishes.

Both the farming venture and the happy little house where the Wilders had started their married life were in ruins.

Manly hastily constructed a shanty for the family to live in near the fire-blackened hole where the house had been. But he and Laura were planning to leave Dakota. Manly had never fully recovered his health, and with the beginning of another drought season, he could see little hope in continued farming. His father's farm in Minnesota was flourishing, and extra help was always needed there. So Manly and Laura decided to make a long visit to Spring Valley in the spring of 1890.

The Wilder sheep were sold for $500. The money went half to the Wilders and half to Peter Ingalls. Manly readied a covered wagon for the trip east. Laura and Manly packed their few possessions and told Rose all about Minnesota, where they were going. Over and over while her parents packed, Rose repeated the syllables, Min-ne-so-ta.

The Wilders said good-bye to Laura's family. As Pa's family had done in Walnut Grove, the Wilders were back-trailing to the East, where they hoped to find life easier.

Laura rode her pony part of the way on the long trip across eastern South Dakota* and Minnesota. Laura and Manly and Rose were welcomed kindly into the big Wilder farmhouse in Spring Valley.

---

*In 1889, the Dakota Territory had been granted statehood, and the land was divided into North and South Dakota.

Laura grew to love Manly's father and mother, who did all they could to make things comfortable for their guests. Rose became a great favorite among the Wilder relatives and friends.

Manly, Laura and Rose spent over a year with the Wilders. Then it was suggested that Manly should try a warmer, milder climate to improve his poor health.

Laura's cousin Peter had settled in Florida, following a trip he had made down the Mississippi. Peter had married a southern girl and lived in the Florida panhandle near a village called Westville. He wrote to the Wilders, praising the warm weather, the pine forests and the opportunities of Florida homesteading. Manly and Laura decided to follow Peter to Florida.

Manly auctioned off his horses, livestock and remaining possessions in Spring Valley, and in the fall of 1891, the Wilders were ready to travel again. They decided to journey by train, which would be Rose's first experience on the railroad. Well supplied with boxes of food and parting presents from the Wilder relatives, Laura and Manly and Rose boarded the train for the South.

Neither Laura nor Manly had ever seen a place

like the Florida backwoods. Gray moss dripped off trees, and scrubby pines grew up from the red-tinged earth. Laura described it as a land "where the trees always murmur, where butterflies are enormous, where plants that eat insects grow in moist places and alligators inhabit the slowly moving water of the rivers. But . . . a Yankee woman was more of a curiosity than any of these."

When the Wilders were settled, the neighbors viewed them with suspicion. Laura was seen as a haughty "up-North gal," and even Cousin Peter's wife disliked her. Laura kept Rose protectively close to her at all times. She concealed a revolver in her skirt pocket for safety.

Perhaps Manly worked in the lumbering camps near Westville, or perhaps he simply rested and tried again to regain his strength. The southern climate made Laura ill. The dampness and heat drained her and made her long for high, level prairies.

After less than a year in Florida, the Wilders decided to go home. They knew that South Dakota was still in a drought cycle. But the homestead land was still there, and friends and family. In August of 1892, they packed their few belongings and boarded the train for home.

Manly, Laura and Rose were welcomed at the Ingalls home. They visited there awhile before they moved into a house a block away. Manly worked when he could, doing carpentry or painting, or clerking in his brother Royal's store. Pa also had a store, called "Ingalls and Company," and sometimes needed help when he drove his peddler's wagon into the countryside to sell to farmers.

Laura found work at the dressmaker's for $1 a day. While her parents worked, Rose spent the day at the Ingalls home. She sat with Ma and Mary in the parlor and learned to knit and sew and drink cambric tea. She was five when she was admitted to the De Smet school and surprised everyone with her talent and enthusiasm for reading and writing.

The Wilders' dream of wheat farming was finished. Manly and Laura talked and planned. They needed to find a climate where intense cold would not plague Manly's crippled feet. They needed to farm on a small scale.

They heard of land developments in the Ozark Mountains of southern Missouri. Land companies circulated glossy pictures of orchards, fat cattle, tree-covered hills and rushing streams. Missouri seemed to be a land of promise.

A neighbor from De Smet went to the Ozarks to look things over. He brought back a Missouri apple and gave it to Laura. It was the biggest, reddest apple she had seen. That apple decided where the Wilder family would settle next.

When their friends heard that the Wilders were moving again, they wondered and worried. The drought would end sometime, they guessed. Why did the Wilders travel so much?

An old school friend of Laura's came to see her. She asked why Laura and Manly were going to Missouri. Laura did not explain all the reasons. She could not bear to tell again all the hardships she and Manly had endured since their marriage. All she could answer was: "We want to see the world!"

11. To the Land of the Big Red Apple

As the spring days lengthened into the summer of 1894, Laura and Manly prepared for the journey to a new home in "The Land of the Big Red Apple." They decided to settle in Mansfield, Missouri, high atop the Ozark hills. Farmland was for sale there, at low prices. While Manly readied the wagon for the long trip, Laura finished her sewing jobs at the dressmaker's. She had carefully saved the daily dollars she earned by sewing. Laura's savings added up to $100. She hid the hundred-dollar bill in her lap writing desk. That money would buy Missouri land.

Laura tried not to worry about the long move to Missouri or the problems there might be in starting a new home. Hadn't Pa and Ma always been cheerful when they tackled a new move? Although she hardly knew how to imagine Mansfield, or what would be there, in her mind it had become "The Promised Land."

So many caravans of traveling folks were passing through De Smet during that summer of 1894 that the town newspaper wrote about them and discussed the problems of "emigrants" on the road. Each sundown, wagons full of dusty, discouraged homeless families stopped wearily in De Smet for the night. They came from north, south, east and west, all with tales of terrible droughts, ruined farms, and poverty. Beggars came door to door, and once Pa gave a nickel to a traveling minstrel who performed with a dancing bear.

Laura was proud. She wanted no one to think of her family as "covered-wagon folks," with no home or destination. They knew where they were going; they weren't just aimlessly wandering the land. They had good horses and a sound wagon and quality folks at home. And when Laura worried about the future, she remembered the hundred-dollar bill.

For their farewell Sunday supper in De Smet, Laura and Manly and Rose ate at Pa and Ma's house. Ma made the meal a special one, and when they finished their pie, Pa asked for his fiddle.

In the deepening summer dusk on the porch of Pa and Ma's house, they sat together one last time: Pa and Ma; Mary, Carrie and Grace; and Laura, Manly and Rose.

That night, Pa's fiddle sang its last concert for Laura, recalling songs from the Big Woods and prairies, musical evenings along the trail in the covered wagon, melodies from the singing school in De Smet and the music of the family's favorite hymns.

Somehow, the fiddle sang what Laura felt but could not say about leaving home. She thought:

> How it had made merry with us when we were
> glad and sympathized with us when we were sad.
> It gave us songs of praise when we had been
> good or successful and acted as confessor when
> we had been bad. Whatever religion, romance
> and patriotism I have I owe largely to the violin
> and Pa playing in the twilight.

When the fiddle played its last notes and it was time to get Rose to sleep for an early-morning start, Pa gave Laura a farewell promise.

"When I'm gone, Laura, when the time comes," Pa told her, "I want you to have the fiddle."

July 17, 1894, was the first date Laura penciled

into a small nickel notebook she kept as a diary of the trip from De Smet to Mansfield. She thought it would be interesting to read about their trek after they were safely settled in a new home in the Ozarks.* Another family from De Smet, the Cooleys, was traveling with the Wilders. Mr. and Mrs. Cooley and their two boys, Paul and George, planned to stop in Mansfield, too. Mr. Cooley had already been there on a trip, just to look over the countryside.

Laura and Manly had filled the black-painted wagon with all it would hold to supply them on the trip south. The hens' coop was fastened to the back of the wagon; they squawked and grumbled at their new home. But Manly said they would soon forget where they were, and it would be good to have fresh eggs to eat on the long drive.

The Wilders and Cooleys traveled together and camped side by side as they drove across the drought-dusty midsummer prairies. From De Smet, they traveled straight south to Yankton, South Dakota, on the Missouri River. As they stopped to cross the muddy yellow river on a ferry, a frighten-

---

*Laura's diary was found after her death and edited by Rose. In 1962 it was published as *On the Way Home*.

ing summer storm brewed at sunset. Black clouds crowded the angry sky, dust gusted into the river and a hard wind shook the wagon, frightening the hens. Manly, Laura and Rose waited anxiously, hoping the ferry operator would let them cross the river to the Nebraska side. A long line of white-topped covered wagons was behind them.

It seemed that South Dakota was jeering at them, angry that they were going. Wind gusts churned the clouds, and suddenly the sunset added an ugly yellow gleam to the fearsome sky. Laura turned to Rose and told her, "That's your last sight of Dakota."

After they crossed the Missouri, the Wilders and the Cooleys moved farther south and east through Nebraska and Kansas. They met many weary travelers. The heat and the dust sometimes made the days unpleasant. Often, Laura recorded in her diary that the temperature exceeded 100 degrees. As it usually did on the plains, the wind blew ceaselessly over the hot, dry land. Sundays were days of rest; they did not travel on that day.

On August 22, Laura noted in her diary that Kansas was behind them. They crossed the Missouri state line, and immediately liked what they saw.

Missouri was hilly, and it was green. The Wilders met a man who assured them that one of the finest farming regions in the world would be around Mansfield. The farther east they traveled, the more rolling the country became. The travelers marveled that they could no longer hear the wind blow the way it did on the prairie. Instead, it gently swayed the trees and sent cool breezes through the moving wagon. Laura remarked in her diary that there were "beautiful, sturdy oak trees on both sides of the road." While the wagon creaked along the roads through the tunnels of arching oaks, Laura was reminded of the long-ago Wisconsin woods.

Laura saw that the Ozarks were not really mountains, nor were they hills. The Ozarks were valleys. The ridgetops were level where they met the blue skyline. Ages ago, streams had cut deep gashes into the Ozark plateau, leaving stony-ledged hillsides, chiseled valleys and ravines. Numberless streams tumbled out of the limestone ledges, and blackberries grew heavy in the thickets. Laura declared: "There is no other country in the world like the Ozarks!"

While the wagons rested at Lamar, Missouri, Laura wrote letters back home to De Smet. She sent one to Carter P. Sherwood, the editor of *The De Smet News and Leader*, thinking he might like to print her reflections on her travels. Laura wrote:

> We have had a very pleasant trip so far, no bad weather to delay us, having had only a few light showers, and those in the night. Our camping places have been delightful. . . . It is a continual picnic for the children to wade in creeks and play in the woods, and sometimes we think we are children and do likewise. We have eaten apples, grapes, plums, and melons until we actually do not care for any more, and to satisfy a Dakota appetite for such things is truly something wonderful. There are hazelnuts, hickory nuts and walnuts along the road, but they are green yet.

Carter Sherwood published Laura's letter in the paper, and Ma sent the clipping to Laura. She saved it always, and in one of the margins she wrote: "First I ever published."

After six weeks of steady driving, on August 31, 1894, the Wilders and the Cooleys reached Mansfield, Missouri. When the wagons rounded the bend into town, Laura said in a voice full of hope: "This is where we stop."

It was. The Wilders camped in the woods at the

edge of Mansfield until they could find a farm. The Cooleys moved into a hotel on the town square; they had been hired as innkeepers.

Manly and Laura looked over many farms, but selecting the right place was a difficult decision. Finally, Laura spied just the place she wanted. It was a rough, rocky forty acres of land, just a mile from the town square in Mansfield. Manly wondered aloud at Laura's immediate attraction to the abandoned, neglected little farm. It did not look like a promising place to him. "I had just left the prairies of South Dakota," he said, "where the land is easily farmed. Coming from such smooth country, the place looked so rough to me that I hesitated to buy it."

Although Manly was doubtful, Laura foresaw that the land could be made both productive and beautiful. She immediately decided the farm needed a name; it was not hard to think of one. Looking around at the flinty, brownish-white stones covering the gullies and sharp ridges, Laura named the land Rocky Ridge Farm.

Manly inquired and learned that the price for the farm was $400—$10 per acre. With the farm came 400 tiny apple trees, waiting to be planted when the land was cleared. The previous owners of the land had ordered those apple trees from a nursery. Then they had thought of the work connected with an orchard and simply abandoned the apple seedlings and the farm. Using the hundred-dollar bill as a down payment, the Wilders bought Rocky Ridge Farm on September 24, 1894, from The Bank of Mansfield.

When the papers were signed at the bank, Manly, Laura and Rose immediately moved out to their new home. A log cabin stood at the edge of a ravine on the property. It was heated by a big rock fireplace, but there were no windows. Laura said after they moved in, "The light in the log house, what there was of it, came down the chimney and through holes in the mud chinking between the logs of the walls. If, for any reason we needed more light, we just punched out some more of the chinking. Light came in that way, but so did the wind and rain!"

Laura, with Rose's help, made the cabin cozy and comfortable for the coming winter. Manly started to work cutting down trees on Rocky Ridge Farm, to clear the land and provide winter fuel.

The Wilders were home.

12. Rocky Ridge Farm

"Our idea of an ideal home is one built by a man and a woman together," Laura said. The Wilders' Rocky Ridge Farm was developed through Laura and Manly working together to transform their Ozark land into a fruit, dairy and poultry farm. Just as they had been partners as wheat farmers in South Dakota, the Wilders were determined to create a successful farm in Missouri. Because Manly was still weakened by his crippled feet, he needed Laura's quickness and energy. She became Manly's best helper.

Through that first winter on Rocky Ridge, Laura and Manly worked to clear the brush and timber from their land. Some of the fallen trees were saved to use as fence rails and for building a log barn and henhouse. Laura loved working in the winter woods, where the gray tree trunks stretched up to the sky and the ground was frosty and hard underfoot. A two-man crosscut saw was used in felling the trees. Laura pulled one end of the saw and Manly pulled the other, and the raspy sound filled the woods.

While Laura and Manly worked in the woods, Rose studied in the red brick school in town. Often, when she walked up the path to the cabin after school, she could hear the ringing of her father's ax from the woods. He cut wagonloads of wood and hauled them into Mansfield to sell for 75 cents a load. That money helped to buy groceries and kerosene during the first months on Rocky Ridge, along with money from the eggs Laura sold. By spring of 1895, twenty acres of land were cleared in time to plant the apple orchard and the first crops.

During spring planting time, Laura and Manly and Rose worked together to sow seed for the corn-field at the head of the ravine. Rose was only eight, but she helped Laura plant the garden seeds and gather the eggs the hens laid in the grasses near the cabin. When huckleberries and blackberries ripened in the woods, Rose picked them for pies or walked into town to sell them for 10 cents a gallon.

At school, Rose Wilder quickly became known

as the smartest pupil in her class. She could spell her way to the head of the line in the Friday spelling contests, and she loved to read. From the library shelves at school, she brought books home to be read aloud by the firelight. While Manly ate his evening bowl of popcorn and Rose worked her arithmetic sums by the light of the kerosene lamp, Laura read to them all. During those evenings by the fire they read *The Leatherstocking Tales*, *Five Little Peppers and How They Grew*, *Pride and Prejudice*, *Ben Hur*, *The House of the Seven Gables* and *Martin Chuzzlewit*. They also liked the suspense of reading serial stories printed in newspapers. Each week a new chapter would appear, and each week the chapter would end abruptly, leaving the Wilders eager to know what would happen next.

Before they had left South Dakota, *The De Smet News and Leader* had started printing a story called "The Rockanock Stage." Rose enjoyed the tale so much that Grandma Ingalls sent each weekly installment on to the Wilders in Missouri after it had been read aloud to Mary. One week, Grandma Ingalls' letter didn't come and Rose wrote immediately, asking for the missing installment. Grace went from house to house on Third Street until she found another copy and mailed it to her eager niece.

On Sundays, after their busy week of work and school, the Wilders drove to town in the buggy to attend services at the Mansfield Methodist Church. Sometimes, they spent the rest of the day at the Cooleys', or the Cooleys came out to Rocky Ridge for the afternoon. If the weather was good, Laura liked to serve picnic dinners in the ravine. While the parents rested along the shady ledges, Rose and Paul and George waded in the creek, ran up and down the steep hills or used the tough grape vines as swings. Laura and Rose enjoyed showing company how they had tamed wild birds and squirrels to eat from their hands.

Manly and Laura still loved horseback riding, and together they rode over the hills of Rocky Ridge or along leaf-shaded roads nearby. They were determined that Rose should learn to ride, so they bought her a fat, stubborn little donkey to start with, named Spookendyke. Rose quickly grew to hate her pet, especially when she was expected to ride him the mile to school and back. Each morning Rose, carrying her dinner pail and books, mounted Spookendyke, but by the time they reached the gate at the bottom of the hill, the determined donkey would balk. He slumped forward, letting Rose, her books and her dinner tumble to the ground. Rose was usually forced to lead Spookendyke to school, where she tied him up, only to listen to his embarrassing squealings while she studied in the quiet classroom.

"He was one of my most hated, if not *the* most hated memories," Rose later said, laughing when she recalled Spookendyke and her trips back and forth to school with him.

By the second summer on Rocky Ridge Farm, the Wilders were cheerfully prospering. They were able to meet the payments on their land and pay the 8 percent interest rates. They bought six more acres for $18; now they had a cow and a pig, and more grazing land was needed. Rose and Laura churned good butter, which sold in town for 10 cents a pound. There were extra vegetables to sell to the townspeople who had no gardens. "We thought we were rich!" Laura said of the second year on the farm.

The stubborn, stony Ozark soil of Rocky Ridge Farm started to produce for the Wilders. Manly and Laura read and studied about the orchard business, and their twenty acres of apple trees grew well. They added peach and pear trees to the orchard and then planted strawberries and raspberries between the tree rows. They built an arbor and planted grapes. On the cleared land, Manly planted fields of oats and corn and wheat. When he looked over the farm and saw the crops growing and smooth, green meadows and pastures, he said, "I can hardly bring my mind back to the rough, rocky, ugly, brushy place we first called Rocky Ridge Farm."

Although they both were interested in every aspect of the farming that was done on Rocky Ridge, Manly and Laura also decided to each select a specialty. Laura chose the poultry; she was always proud that selling her chickens and eggs during the first winter on the farm had helped buy needed food and supplies from town. Manly decided that he would handle the cows; he said that Rocky Ridge was a natural dairy farm, with much good, clear spring water available and good grazing grass growing where the trees were cleared. When he and Laura bought another forty acres to add to the farm, there was plenty of land for a herd of cattle.

While they were expanding the farm, the Wilders also enlarged the cabin at the edge of the ravine. After their first winter in the tiny log house, Manly added a frame room with real windows and a door. And in the spring of 1896, he and Laura selected a new building site, a few steps from the cabin but still on the ravine's edge. They removed the new frame room from the old cabin and rolled the room on big logs to the new site, leaving the cabin to be used as a barn. Then Manly built a new room and joined the two rooms together, with a sleeping loft above for Rose. That was the beginning of the new house on Rocky Ridge Farm.

Once the Wilders became acquainted with their neighbors, there were country cornhusking parties and frolics and barn dances and quilting bees to attend. In the summer there were outdoor singings and play parties to enjoy. Laura loved dancing. "There is always a little music in my feet," she explained. At parties, when the fiddlers and banjo players tuned up for "Sweet Betsy from Pike" or "Ta-ra-ra-boom-de-ay" or "There'll Be a Hot Time in the Old Town Tonight," Laura was ready to dance.

The food at the Ozark gatherings the Wilders attended during those early years was always bountiful. Long boards covered with tablecloths held so many baskets and bowls and platters that no space remained uncovered. Laura's own specialty for parties was her gingerbread, made from an old recipe she'd learned from Ma. Whenever there was a dinner, or the Methodist church ladies were planning a social, Laura was asked to bring a pan of spicy gingerbread. At home, Laura saved the gingerbread for special occasions: Thanksgiving, Christmas, Rose's December birthday, or her own birthday or Manly's, both of which were in February.

Rose was ambitious to make the gingerbread recipe and she never forgot her first experience baking it. It was Manly's birthday and he and Laura were gone for the day. Rose had been given permission to bake the birthday gingerbread, even though, as she remembered it, "My mother had often left me to watch the bread baking and every time she did it I was lost in a book until she rushed into the full-of-smoke house and snatched cinders of loaves out of the oven." But Rose was proud that her mother, whom she called "Mama Bess," trusted her with the gingerbread. She was determined to be especially careful baking her first gingerbread.

I was excited of course and nervous but I made the gingerbread carefully, measuring everything and watching its baking. The gingerbread baked perfectly and I had just taken it out of the oven when the minister came to call. All the duties of hostess were mine unexpectedly, and I felt important. I welcomed the minister, seated him in the front room, spoke politely about the weather and such, then excused myself for a minute and returned with napkins, glasses of water, and three pieces of the hot gingerbread, proudly served. The minister was surprised and pleased. He looked slightly startled at first but ate a piece slowly. He declined a second and soon left. I ate none myself, saving it for the special supper that evening. I would not have cut it for anyone but such a caller as the minister. After supper, my father, my mother and I each took a piece of that beautiful soft, red-brown gingerbread, as tempting as any my mother had baked . . . but it burned, it seemed to blister our tongues! I had used hot cayenne pepper, by mistake, instead of ginger.

The Methodist minister may have been an exception, for visitors who came to Rocky Ridge left the Wilder home with memories of tasty food and interesting talk and the sight of a prosperous farm being carved out of the Ozark land. "Good health, good homes, a good living, good times and good neighbors," Laura said as she thought of their life on Rocky Ridge Farm during the first years in the Ozarks. "What more could anyone want?" she wondered.

Laura at age 70, in 1937, as she looked when *On the Banks of Plum Creek* was published.
(By permission of Laura Ingalls Wilder Home Association)

Laura and Almanzo with Ben the bulldog, at home on Rocky Ridge in the 1940s.
(By permission of Laura Ingalls Wilder Home Association)

Laura signing books in Springfield, Missouri, in 1952.
She was 85.

(By permission of Laura Ingalls Wilder Home Association)

Laura at home on Rocky Ridge, in one of her favorite
velvet dresses. She was 87 when this photo was taken in 1954.

(By permission of Laura Ingalls Wilder Home Association)

Laura with her friend and driver Jim Hartley, and her new
1954 Oldsmobile.

(Hartley family collection)

Pa's fiddle, now on display at the Laura Ingalls Wilder
Home and Museum in Mansfield.

(Photo © 1992 Leslie A. Kelly)

Laura's lap desk, made
by Almanzo and brought
from De Smet to
Mansfield in 1894.
(Photo © 1992
Leslie A. Kelly)

The oval glass bread plate
that survived the fire in
the Wilder tree-claim
house in De Smet.
(Photo © 1992
Leslie A. Kelly)

Almanzo gave this striking clock to Laura for a Christmas surprise in 1886. For the rest of his life, he wound the clock just before bedtime. It is still ticking in the Wilder home on Rocky Ridge Farm.
(Photo © 1992 Leslie A. Kelly)

The Ingalls family Bible, now on display at the Laura Ingalls Wilder Home and Museum in Mansfield.
(Photo © 1992 Leslie A. Kelly)

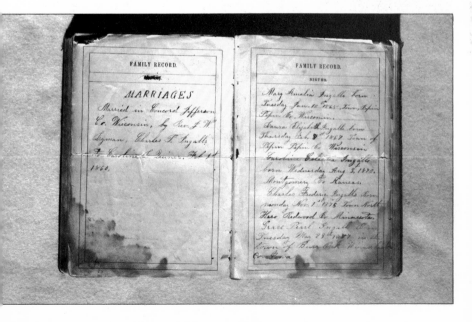

The rock house that Rose had built for Almanzo and Laura in 1928.
(By permission of Laura Ingalls Wilder Home Association)

13. The Gem City of the Ozarks

S oon after the Wilders arrived there, the town of Mansfield experienced a small boom. A new railroad line encouraged small industries to begin and helped to bring families to the area. Mining activity also brought people to town. The Berry Mine near Mansfield shipped out ore to St. Louis, and the Lead Hill mining operation produced zinc and lead.

During the late 1890's, downtown Mansfield was a busy place. Around the town square, fancy brick buildings were constructed to house various businesses. There were general stores, a bakery, a drugstore, an opera house for traveling shows, flour mills and a bank. The square was filled with shade trees and it was a good place to watch town activities and to await the arrival of freight and passenger trains at the depot. Traveling salesmen often stepped off the train with their sample cases and headed for the stores, or went to one of the two hotels in town.

The Mansfield newspaper bragged about the town, calling it "one of the best and most prosperous cities in this part of the state. Mansfield is the 'Gem City of the Ozarks' in every sense of the word." At the edge of town, on the road out to Rocky Ridge Farm, stood a little yellow frame house. It was one story, with an attic above and a front porch decorated with lacy wooden scrollwork. It was close to the school and it was less than a mile from the Wilder farm. In 1898, Manly and Laura decided to rent the house for $5 a month and try living in town. They knew that years would pass before Rocky Ridge was a self-supporting farm, and they wanted to earn money to invest in their land. Mansfield seemed to be the best place for them to live while they established their farm.

Manly Wilder became Mansfield's drayman. Mr. Cooley had started a hauling and draying service soon after the Cooleys and the Wilders settled in Mansfield. In those days before automobiles, each town needed a deliveryman whose team and wagon could haul loads in town and country. When Mr. Cooley died, Manly bought the business and the team and wagon from Mrs. Cooley.

As a drayman, Manly met the trains at the depot and unloaded shipments of merchandise for the stores. Laura and Rose were always the first to know when new styles or fresh bolts of material arrived. They also knew who came and went on the train. When travelers or railroad workers or salesmen wanted a good meal, Manly suggested his own house. Laura had started cooking and serving meals in the little yellow house as a way to earn extra money.

Laura's cooking quickly became profitable. She decided not to cook in "city style," but instead to serve "things nearly impossible to get in the city." These included fresh eggs, new milk, fruits, vegetables and frying chickens raised on Rocky Ridge and brought into town. Laura discovered that she could earn extra cash "by using home products, combining with them a spirit of hospitality and a little taking of thought." Laura also enjoyed the interesting people she often met at her table. One of them was Mr. N. J. Craig, who worked at The Bank of Mansfield. He became one of the Wilders' closest friends.

Living in Mansfield made Rose a "town girl," definitely an improvement from riding Spookendyke to and from the farm when she went to school. The year the family moved to town, Rose was eleven and in the "Sixth Reader" class. Rose read constantly; one of the Wilders' neighbors had a wall of books, and Rose borrowed and read them all.

The Mansfield school extended only to the eighth grade, and Rose longed to continue her schooling. Some of her schoolmates planned to attend private academies in larger towns, where high school courses were offered. But Rose knew the academies charged tuition that her parents could not afford.

During the summer of 1898, the Wilders had their first visit from relatives. Manly's parents, Rose's Grandpa and Grandma Wilder, along with his oldest sister Laura, arrived for a long stay. Laura was then a widow traveling with her parents. They were moving to Crowley, Louisiana, where Manly's brother Perley and sister Eliza Jane had settled. Eliza Jane had married a wealthy rice plantation owner and had a son named Wilder. She was convinced the entire Wilder family should move to Louisiana.

Grandpa Wilder was eighty-five when he sold his beautiful Spring Valley farm for several thousand dollars. Eliza Jane and Perley talked him into investing most of his money in Louisiana rice lands and then invited him and Grandma to live in Crowley. Royal Wilder had married and settled in Spring Valley as a merchant, and he refused to move south. Manly had worked so hard making his start in Mansfield that he would not leave. Besides, neither he nor Laura were fond of Eliza Jane, who had been Laura's teacher back in De Smet.

During the weeks they spent in Mansfield, the older Wilders often worried about the money they had invested in rice farming. Both Grandma and Grandpa feared that their money would be lost, though Manly tired to reassure them. One day as their visit was ending, Grandpa surprised Manly. He had bought the rented house on the edge of town and turned over the deed to his son.

Grandpa and Grandma Wilder and Manly's sister Laura continued south, only to find that most of their fortune had been lost in poor investments. Grandpa died in a few months, homesick for his

Minnesota home but content that he had provided one for Manly in Missouri.

Laura's family back in South Dakota often wrote with news of friends and happenings in De Smet. Pa and Ma were comfortable in their house on Third Street. Mary lived with them, busy with her Braille books, her music, her handwork and church activities. She was cheerful and happy and a great help to Ma with the housework.

Carrie worked at *The De Smet News and Leader* office for many years, and also lived with Ma and Pa. Her wages helped support the Ingalls home, but she found time to enjoy her bicycle, tennis, church work and ladies' clubs in De Smet.

Grace took a college teaching course and became a country schoolteacher, just as Laura had done. She taught several schools west of De Smet, in the Manchester area, and while there met a farmer named Nate Dow. Grace and Nate were married in the parlor of Pa and Ma's home in October 1901. Their own home was a farm on the prairie seven miles west of De Smet.

In the winter and spring following Grace's marriage, the letters from De Smet were filled with concern over Pa. He was sixty-six and suffering from heart failure. In May 1902, the message came that Laura should come home. Pa was dying.

In haste, Laura left the housework to fifteen-year-old Rose. Laura boarded trains and changed trains all the way to South Dakota. Finally, her train stopped at De Smet. There was no fiddle music to greet her homecoming, but Laura had arrived in time to see Pa once more. He lingered until June 8, dying with Ma and their four daughters close by.

Pa's music, his kindness, his respect for hard work and his sparkling blue eyes and cheerfulness had always influenced Laura, even through her first hard years of married life and later when she and Manly had established their new home in the Ozarks. At Pa's funeral in the Congregational church, his favorite hymn was sung: "Sweet By and By." Laura thought that when her time came to die, perhaps Pa and his fiddle might be playing that song for her.

Laura lingered in De Smet to visit with her family. When she left, it was the last time she ever saw Ma and Mary. They lived on together for many years in the cozy house Pa had built but never visited Mansfield. Carrie visited the Wilders in 1903 and was so impressed with the Ozarks that she

bought a lot in the town of Mansfield as an investment.

During the summer of 1903, Manly's sister Eliza
Jane and her son Wilder came to visit Mansfield.
Eliza Jane was now a widow, and she had spoiled
Wilder rotten. Manly and Laura were speechless at
some of Wilder's actions, such as purposely break-
ing their sitting-room window. Rose was amazed at
her younger cousin's bold and fearless behavior.
They became great friends that summer. When
Eliza Jane and Wilder were preparing to return
home to Louisiana, they asked Rose to join them.
Rose longed to attend a real high school and study
Latin, which she could do if she lived in Crowley
with her aunt.

Manly and Laura agreed that Rose could spend
a year away from home, so she left Mansfield along
with her aunt and cousin. In Crowley, Rose was a
brilliant student, just as she had been in Mansfield.
She passed the high school entrance examinations
easily because she had read so widely at home.

And during the year in Crowley, Rose crammed
four years' worth of Latin into one. When she grad-
uated in the spring of 1904, Rose addressed the audience at commencement exercises with an original

Latin poem she had composed. As Eliza Jane said, Rose was a "very bright girl."

When Rose returned to Mansfield, she saw that her parents were no closer to their goal of making Rocky Ridge Farm a paying farm than they had been when she left. Manly had become a salesman for an oil company, delivering kerosene, oil, stove gas and turpentine all over the countryside.

The Wilders rented out the house on Rocky Ridge, but they kept working to improve the farm. After he finished his delivery route, Manly tended the crops, the orchard and the livestock on the farm. Sometimes a hired man helped him with the work.

Rose could see no way to help her parents financially. There was no work for a young girl in Mansfield, no chance that she could attend college. She had no moneymaking skills. But then Rose found a way to learn telegraphy. The Mansfield depotmaster agreed to teach both his daughter and Rose the language of the telegraph key. Rose caught on quickly. When she was ready, she found a job in Kansas City, Missouri, as a telegraph operator. The pay was $2.50 per week—enough to support herself and perhaps to send money home. At seventeen, Rose left Mansfield.

When Rose left home, the era of the working woman had just started. Employed women were called "bachelor girls" and were considered very modern. One of the first things Rose did in Kansas City was to shorten her skirts to keep them above the dirty sidewalks. Then she cut her long hair. Both styles created a stir in Mansfield on Rose's visits home.

Although they worked hard in town and on the farm, Laura and Manly were happy during the years when they lived in the little yellow frame house. They worked on projects at the Methodist church, where Laura organized the first Christmas bazaar. Almanzo was active in the Masonic Lodge in Mansfield, and both he and Laura were members of the Eastern Star organization. They liked the religious and charitable ideals of the Stars and Masons. With friends, they enjoyed parties, socials, picnics, fishing trips and campouts.

Of the Mansfield years, Laura later said, "We worked hard, but it was interesting and didn't hurt us any."

14. "As a Farm Woman Thinks"

Laura and Manly spent more than a decade working and living in town. They weathered the financial Panic of 1907, and they inherited $500 from Manly's parents. Then they decided to sell their town house and finish the partially completed home on Rocky Ridge Farm.

Laura had dreamed for years about an ideal farm home. She imagined it rising from the land, constructed of materials found on the farm. Rock for the foundation, fireplace and chimney abounded on the Wilder farm; timber was all around. When she dreamed her dreams aloud to Manly, he simply said, "Draw the plans!"

Laura planned with pencil and paper and laid out additions to the existing little house, until she had designed a ten-room farmhouse, including four porches, a beamed parlor, a rock fireplace, a library, and an open stairway to the upstairs. Manly looked at the plans and started preparing timber. In 1911, logs were cut, hauled to the mill, sawed and piled to season and dry for a year.

The renters left the two-room house on Rocky Ridge and the Wilders crowded in with their belongings. The kitchen was filled with pantry items. The "front room" was crowded with an organ, a desk, a table, chairs and a bed. A narrow staircase led up to the attic room and there Laura stored the sofa and her clothing.

The Wilders were farming full-time, and Manly was busy in the fields and in the orchard. He hired a stonemason to lay the rock foundation and a carpenter to frame the new house. The workmen came and tore off the old roof just in time for a rainstorm to ruin the new spring clothes Laura had put in the attic. During the racket, Laura tended her garden and her hens and served good noon meals to the workmen. She knew that her food must be delicious and she must be cheerful, or the workers would simply wander off to work for more "neighborly" folks, leaving the job undone.

Between his farm work and planning with the workmen, Manly hauled rocks from the fields and hollows of the farm for the foundation and chimney. When he found fossils imbedded in the brown and white rocks, he saved them to use as facing on the chimney. Finally, Manly had had enough. He told Laura he would haul no more rock. Instead, he brought a load of red brick from town to use for the fireplace.

Laura was determined to have a native rock fireplace. "I objected strenuously," she said. "I argued; I begged; and at last when everything failed I wept." To her surprise, tears softened Manly. The fireplace was constructed of an enormous slab of Ozark rock at the top, supported by two equally sturdy stones found on the farm.

Oak lumber came from the country sawmill rough-cut, and it had to be hand finished. Laura wanted the oak to be finished in its natural color and used to panel the big parlor. Though she had never seen a beamed ceiling, she wanted one. And she wanted windows.

Great clear sheets of glass were placed in the parlor walls, to bring the view of the land and trees and sky inside. Laura said the windows were her pictures, and they were constantly changing for her.

In one corner of the parlor, near the fireplace, was a little library made of five-foot shelves. Laura kept her books there, and the stacks of *Adventure Magazine* that she saved. On the wall she hung Rose's big graduation picture from Crowley.

Opposite the library was a cozy little dining alcove, convenient to the kitchen. Through a door was Laura's small office, where she could sit at her desk to write letters and keep the farm's account books. The office was connected with the long bedroom used by Laura and Manly. The parlor stairway led from the parlor to two rooms and a sleeping porch upstairs.

Laura's farm kitchen was also her workplace. She not only cooked the meals there, but she also did all the canning and preserving of fruits and vegetables. She churned in the kitchen, baked bread, cleaned the kerosene lamps each morning and prepared food for the pigs and hens. To keep her kitchen tidy, Manly built in cupboards and drawers so that everything from the kerosene can to the churn would have a place to be stored out of sight. A little room was built off the kitchen for a woodshed.

The sturdy oak-framed farmhouse was covered with pine siding and painted white with gray trim. It stood under the shady oaks on the green land, almost a part of the landscape. "It seems to belong on the low hill where it stands," Laura observed, "with the tree-covered mountain at its back."

When the house on Rocky Ridge Farm was finally complete in the fall of 1913, it was a showplace of the Ozarks. The Wilder home was unique, and visitors often did not know how to compliment it. The remark that Laura appreciated the most came from a friend. "You have expressed yourself!" she said. "It fits you as though it were your shell."

Beyond the finished house was the flourishing farm. Apples and pears and peaches were packed in barrels to be sold in town or shipped to markets in Memphis and St. Louis. Strawberries and raspberries grew on the slopes all around. Corn and wheat brought good prices at harvest time. "The soil repays bountifully the care given it," Laura explained when visitors remarked on the Wilders' fruitful acres.

Manly watched over his herd of white-faced Jersey cows with special pride. He kept track of the amounts of milk the cows produced and carefully noted the cost of feed. Laura recorded how much money they received when they delivered dairy products to Mansfield's creamery.

Laura's specialty on the farm was a flock of flighty Leghorn hens. She designed a convenient henhouse that was clean and airy. She supplied plenty of fresh water for the hens. She fed the flock well, but economically, for Laura's goal was to make a dollar profit per hen over the hen's lifetime. Most of the hen feed was grown on Rocky Ridge.

Laura's success as a poultry raiser became known throughout the Ozarks. One neighbor marveled that "in the winter, she gets eggs, when *no one* gets eggs!" Invitations arrived for Laura to appear at farmers' meetings to share her ideas and methods.

Once when Laura was too busy at home to present a talk, she sent a speech to be read in her absence. In the audience that day was John Case, the editor of the farm weekly *The Missouri Ruralist*. He was so impressed by Laura's writing style that he invited her to submit articles for publication.

Laura was both pleased and bashful when Mr. Case requested her writings. She had little formal training, but she had always loved to read and study words. So Laura decided to try. Her first article, titled "Favors the Small Farm Home," appeared in the *Ruralist's* pages in February 1911. Laura turned forty-four that month and started her career as a writer.

Between farm chores and housework, Laura wrote. She did interviews with country people; she wrote essays and poems; she researched long feature stories. Some of her writing dealt with happenings on Rocky Ridge Farm. When Laura wrote about Manly, she referred to him as "The Man of the Place." Throughout all of Laura's writing, her message was simple: Country life was good.

The writing of "Mrs. A. J. Wilder," as she was called in the *Ruralist*, became a steady feature for many years. Laura was proud when readers wrote to praise her and when an editor told her, "Frankly, Mrs. Wilder, I like you and your stories better than anything that reaches us."

The money paid to Laura for her articles was not much, ranging from $5 to $10. The *Ruralist* gave her a column called "The Farm Home" and, later, one called "As a Farm Woman Thinks." She also served as the *Ruralist's* Household Editor.

Laura Wilder became known as an expert on farm life. She contributed articles about poultry to the St. Louis *Star Farmer* and sold feature stories about the Ozarks to the *St. Louis Post-Dispatch* and the *Kansas City Star*.

While Laura and Manly were building up Rocky Ridge Farm, Rose was a big-city career woman. As a Western Union telegrapher she traveled widely, finally settling in San Francisco. She and Gillette Lane were married there in 1909. Soon after their wedding, the Lanes moved to Kansas City to work. Rose was employed as a writer for the *Kansas City Post*.

Laura wrote to Rose:

> When your brain is tired and heart is sore,
> With longing to be free,
> Then turn away from the crowds of men
> And come to the woods with me.

It was an easy train trip from Kansas City to Mansfield, so Rose and Gillette did come to Rocky Ridge. Laura and Manly liked Gillette Lane. The farm became a haven for Rose during the summer of 1910; she came there to recover from the death of her baby son. Like Laura, Rose had given birth to an infant boy who did not live.

The traveling spirit seemed to be as strong in Rose as it was in Laura and Manly. She and Gillette returned to California where they had a busy joint career selling real estate. Rose was one of the first female land agents in northern California. She sold millions of acres of farmland and was successful until the threat of World War I slowed sales. Then a friend asked Rose to help with the writing for the women's page of the *San Francisco Bulletin*. By 1915, Rose Wilder Lane was an established *Bulletin* journalist.

Back at Rocky Ridge, Laura was struggling to expand her writing. Rose advised her to find someone else to tend hens and to concentrate on her writing. Through letters, Laura and Rose exchanged writing ideas, discussed possible stories and sought ways for Laura to sell her writing to higher-paying publications than the *Missouri Ruralist*.

Laura was awed by Rose's success in San Francisco. Rose interviewed celebrities such as businessman Henry Ford, the actor Charlie Chaplin and daredevil airplane pilot Art Smith. Laura was eager to learn more of Rose's writing techniques. In 1915, the year of the San Francisco World's Fair, Rose invited her Mama Bess to visit. "I simply can't stand being homesick for you any more," Rose wrote.

Laura was reluctant to leave Manly with all the farmwork. But when Rose offered to help with expenses, Laura decided to go. With Manly urging her on, Laura made the train trip from Mansfield to San Francisco. She spent two months there, visiting Rose and Gillette, seeing the exciting Fair, meeting Rose's writer and artist friends and pondering over writing ideas. Laura wrote Manly faithfully, and told him that "I intend to do some writing that will count." (Manly saved all the letters Laura wrote from San Francisco. In 1974 they were published as *West From Home*.)

Rose not only wanted to coach Laura in writing; she wanted her parents to move to California. Laura looked over the possibilities of chicken farming there, but she confided to Manly that she wouldn't trade all of California "for one Ozark hill."

Before she left for home, Laura received instructions from the *Ruralist* to write articles about the Missouri exhibits at the Fair. She gathered her material and returned to Rocky Ridge full of enthusiasm and ideas for continuing her journalism career.

15. "Good Times on the Farm!"

"We who live in quiet places," Laura wrote in the *Ruralist*, "have the opportunity to become acquainted with ourselves, to think our own thoughts and live our own lives." Her experience in San Francisco increased her love for Rocky Ridge Farm. The turning seasons, the years filled with the rhythm of growth and harvest, gave both Laura and Manly satisfaction. Rocky Ridge Farm grew to nearly two hundred acres, and the Wilders were proud that they had built it together.

Rose worried that her parents worked too hard. She suggested that they move to St. Louis, take jobs and retire to a country home when they were old. "Well," Laura said, "this farm *is* a country place. We can move to St. Louis and work hard fifteen years or so, save our money and then have a country place. Or we can stay here and keep on working hard enjoying the country place as we go along and then have it."

Laura's contentment in the country became one of her favorite themes in her *Ruralist* columns. She was eager to show readers the beauty she and Manly had discovered in the Ozarks. "A moment's pause to watch the glory of a sunrise or a sunset is soul-satisfying," she wrote, "while a bird's song will set the steps to music all day long."

Laura's message to country women encouraged them to become active partners on family farms. As women across America marched and demanded equality with men, Laura was amused. She realized that "farm women have always been wage earners and partners in their husband's businesses, but no one ever noticed it."

Through her *Ruralist* writing, Laura became active with the Missouri Home Development Association, which worked to improve country life. She felt sympathy for isolated farm women who seldom came to town. When they did travel to the Ozark villages, often there was no place for them to rest or socialize while their husbands did business. Laura successfully worked for the establishment of rest rooms, circulating libraries and social events for country women. She personally organized the women's groups in Mansfield and several other nearby towns. When telephone lines stretched into the country, the Wilders installed a phone on Rocky Ridge, making Laura's organizational work easier to accomplish.

In 1916, Laura helped found a group called The Athenians. It was formed to provide educational experiences and friendship among the members, and had as a goal the creation of a county library. Most of the meetings were held at Hartville, the county seat, and they were very organized. Members were expected to research and present programs for the monthly meetings.

Laura wrote the Athenians' club song, and enthusiastically studied and reported. She especially enjoyed presenting literary programs, telling of Shakespeare, Dickens, Scott and Twain. Manly drove Laura the eleven miles to Hartville in the buggy. While she was busy with the meetings, he sat and played checkers with friends in the hardware store.

In 1917, Laura was able to expand her efforts to improve the life of Ozark farm people. That year, seven farmers organized the Mansfield Farm Loan Association. The loan association enabled farmers to borrow money to buy or improve land through the Federal Land Bank in St. Louis. Interest rates were low and Laura encouraged many of the Wilders' neighbors to do business with the association. Laura served as secretary-treasurer, the only paid position. She interviewed borrowers in her little den in the farmhouse, and later in an office in Mansfield. Helpfully, she explained the forms and applications to clients. Through the years, Laura doled out nearly a million dollars in loans. Periodically, bank examiners from Washington arrived to inspect Laura's records, and she always received high praise for her accuracy.

The Wilders of Mansfield were well-known throughout the Ozarks for their activities, and Rose's reputation as a writer added to her parents' renown. Rose had divorced Gillette in 1918, but still used the name Rose Wilder Lane in her writing. She published a book called *Henry Ford's Own Story* and then wrote her first novel, *Diverging*

ORCHARD

HEN
HOUSE

N

Rocky Ridge Farm, circa 1924

Roads. Her magazine articles gained national attention. When she came to Mansfield to visit, the newspaper called her "a writer of great note" and a "distinguished visitor." Laura held welcoming parties in the parlor for Rose, and proudly took her to Athenian meetings where Rose was often asked to present programs on her experiences in San Francisco and in New York where she had lived in 1919.

In 1920, Rose sailed for France, to work in the Paris publicity office of the American Red Cross. She also dispatched magazine and newspaper reports about conditions in Europe and the Near East following World War I. Postcards, letters and gifts, all stamped with exotic postmarks, were continually received at Rocky Ridge. Budapest, Athens, London, Vienna and Prague were among Rose's stops. A visit to Albania in 1922 and a dangerous trek into the country's highlands became the subject of Rose's book *Peaks of Shala,* which she dedicated "To my mother, Laura Ingalls Wilder."

Laura and Manly missed Rose during her long absences from America, but were thrilled with her long descriptive letters telling of her adventures. Rose was still concerned at the work load on Rocky

Ridge, and begged her parents to rest and hire help. Her writings were bringing Rose a fine income, and she started sending an annual gift of $500 to help with expenses on Rocky Ridge.

Finally, after nearly four years of world travel, Rose came home. Her train from New York came chugging into the Mansfield station in time for Christmas 1923. Manly was there with the lumber wagon to collect Rose's trunks and baggage, but Laura and Rose rode out to the farm in a taxi. There was a fire in the fireplace and chicken pie for dinner.

Old friends dropped in to hear Rose's adventurous tales of travel. Parties were held at Rocky Ridge to welcome her home. Once, Laura rolled up the parlor rugs and engaged fiddlers and callers for an old-fashioned square dance. Another time, she held a costume party and lit the parlor with candles.

Rose's New York and San Francisco friends came to visit Rocky Ridge, bringing excitement to Mansfield. Cheery Helen Boylston, a war nurse whom Rose had met in Poland, arrived for a visit that lasted for over a year. She was nicknamed "Troub" because she seemed to attract trouble. Troub rode horseback nearly every day, and through Rose's influence she became a writer. Her most famous books were the "Sue Barton, Student Nurse" series.

Rose set up her typewriter in the sleeping porch on the second floor of the Rocky Ridge farmhouse. She busily wrote articles and short stories for *The Country Gentleman, Harper's* and *Good Housekeeping*. She wrote a book based on the life of Jack London titled *He Was a Man* and planned an Ozark book called *Hill Billy*.

Rose's goal was to earn enough money to allow Laura and Manly to retire from farming. Her own dream was to return to live in Albania.

One of Rose's many gifts to her Papa and her Mama Bess was a blue 1923 Buick. It was shipped from New York, and Mansfield was full of excitement the day the Buick was unloaded from a railroad car. Rose taught Manly to drive immediately, and he liked it. Laura also learned quickly, but eventually decided to let Manly do all the driving.

In the fall of 1925, Laura, Rose and Troub set out on a trip to California. The Buick, which the Wilders named Isabelle, took them across Kansas, Colorado, Utah, Nevada and California, until they reached San Francisco. Laura enjoyed seeing many of Rose's literary friends in California.

After the California trip, Laura was inspired to resume her writing. Her contributions to the *Ruralist* had dwindled, and she resigned from her job with the Farm Loan Association after almost ten years. Watching Rose work upstairs, reading her published stories and seeing the checks she received for her work encouraged Laura to pursue her own ideas for publication. In 1919, Rose had helped her with an article for *McCall's Magazine*. In 1925, Rose collaborated with Laura again on two articles for *The Country Gentleman*: "My Ozark Kitchen" and "The Farm Dining Room." Laura was well paid. "Mama Bess is very much pleased," Rose noted.

Rose was eager to teach Laura how to write more material for high-paying magazines. "Here is your chance," she said. "to make a real income." She urged Laura to hire out the increasingly difficult farm work, and to concentrate on writing.

Laura and Rose's focus on writing was again interrupted in 1926. Rose and Troub left Rocky Ridge, first to study languages at the Sorbonne in Paris and then to live in Tirana, the capital city of Albania. Letters passed between Laura and Rose, but Laura made no progress with her literary work.

When Rose returned to the farm in 1928, she saw that the work of Rocky Ridge was too heavy for her parents. Manly was seventy-one; Laura was sixty-one. The paralysis in Manly's feet seemed to be creeping up his legs; it was time for him to retire. Laura scolded him until he found a man named Bruce Prock to do most of the farm work. Bruce brought his family to Rocky Ridge to live in a new house the Wilders built across the road from their home. He became a good friend and helper. Laura told Manly just to boss Bruce, and to let him do all the work.

Troub Boylston returned to live in the farmhouse with the Wilders. Other friends came for long visits, so the big old house actually seemed crowded. When Rose sold her Ozark serial called "Cindy" to *The Country Gentleman* for $10,000, she knew what she would do with the money.

Rose decided to build a new house for Manly and Laura. Across the ridge from the old house, a wooded knoll was a perfect spot for the new house. It could easily be reached by a footpath from the farmhouse.

Through the fall of 1928, Manly and Rose supervised the work of the builders. The house was an English-style five-room cottage. It was built of brown and tan rock, with a slate roof. Modern and unusual, the house became a famous place even before the Wilders moved in, with people driving by to look and talk about it.

By late December, the house was completed. New furniture arrived from a department store in Springfield, fifty miles away. On Christmas morning, Rose gave the house key to her Mama Bess and her Papa. Once again, they lived in a little house, this time under the spreading oak and walnut trees of Rocky Ridge Farm.

Rose had the old farmhouse wired for electricity and put away the kerosene lamps for good. The house was freshly painted and furnished to Rose's taste, and she settled in to write. Although Troub spent most of her days enjoying herself horseback riding and going to fox hunts, she too did some writing at Rocky Ridge.

"It seems impossible to me that I have seen so many changes in living," Laura remarked, when she thought of her new home, the Buick that took her and Manly all over the Ozarks and the putting aside of old ways. "Every year has held more interest than the year before," she admitted. As she wrote in *The Missouri Ruralist*, the Wilders were living "good times on the farm!"

16. "Stories That Had to Be Told"

Not long after the Wilders were settled in the rock house, they made the last payment on the land they had farmed for thirty-five years. "Now the place is *ours*," they declared. Rose said that Rocky Ridge Farm, with its three modern houses, pastures, cleared fields and woodlots, rivaled any country estate she had seen in Europe. But, she told her parents, "The farm deserves a rest, and so do you."

One of Manly's last farming ventures was a flock of sheep. When they were sold, he kept busy gardening, woodworking, whittling and pursuing a new interest, a herd of white-faced goats. Sometimes he drove to the pool room in town to chat and play pool. He attended auctions and farm sales and watched Bruce Prock drive the tractor and use newfangled machinery on the land. Wherever he went, Manly was popular. He was witty and jolly, full of stories and keen advice about horses and farming and politics. He and Laura were loyal Democrats until the 1930's.

While Manly kept himself busy, Laura decided to write her autobiography. She thought over her girlhood in the woods and on the prairies with Pa and Ma and her sisters. In fifty short years, the frontier had vanished. Laura believed that her experiences were "altogether too good to be lost." She said they were "stories that had to be told."

In 1930, Laura opened a blue-lined school tablet and started drafting her story in pencil. She began with her family's move to Indian Territory and wrote the story of her life until her wedding to Manly. She titled her manuscript *Pioneer Girl*, and when she completed it, she walked over to the farmhouse and handed it to Rose.

Rose was busy with her own work. But she did as Laura wanted her to. She typed the penciled pages of *Pioneer Girl* and gave her suggestions on the writing.

George Bye was a New York agent who handled Rose's writings, so *Pioneer Girl* was sent to him in hopes that he could sell it to a publisher. Everyone agreed that Laura's book was a fascinating American story, but no editor would buy it. On a visit to New York, Rose herself tried to place *Pioneer Girl* with magazines as a serial. Again, no one accepted it.

Berta Hader, an old San Francisco friend of Rose's, heard of Laura's manuscript. Berta and her husband Elmer were writing and illustrating children's books, and they thought Laura's work could become a children's picture book. Again, it was passed from editor to editor, and finally the children's book department at Harper & Brothers, Publishers, became interested.

Laura rewrote her material into a book about her memories of living in the Big Woods of Wisconsin. She included many of Pa's stories, because she wanted so much to share them with children. Her new attempt was titled *Little House in the Big Woods*. In 1931, Harper & Brothers agreed to publish the book.

In June of 1931, while her first book was in the making, Laura and Manly made a trip to South Dakota. They drove the Buick over the same route they had traveled to Missouri by wagon thirty-seven years earlier. The Middle West was in another drought cycle, so the trip was hot and dusty. Nero, the Wilders' Airedale dog, rode on the running board of the car. Often, it was necessary to stop to give him water or an ice cream cone.

When Laura and Manly arrived in De Smet, they found a modern little town. They drove seven miles west and stopped in Manchester, where Grace and Nate lived. Ma had died in 1924 and Mary in 1928, so Grace was the only Ingalls left in the area.

The Wilders drove over the prairie, visiting Spirit Lake, Pa's homestead, De Smet and their old farm. "Country looks as it used to," Laura noted. They found no buildings on their tree claim, and just a few of the trees left. A grain field grew over the hill on the homestead where Rose had been born. "It all makes me miss those who are gone, Pa and Ma and Mary and the Boasts and Cap Garland," Laura mourned.

Laura and Grace spent a morning going through Ma's and Mary's belongings, which were stored in a room of the Ingalls house. The house was rented out, and they found that "everything of value left there has disappeared." After visiting with old friends in De Smet, the Wilders drove west across South Dakota to the Black Hills, where Carrie lived.

Carrie had married a Black Hills mine owner named David Swanzey and they lived at Keystone, a little town at the foot of Mount Rushmore. Carrie welcomed Laura and Manly and they all went on a tour of the Black Hills in the Wilders' car. They chatted and reminisced as they drove through the pine forest and rock formations.

Laura called South Dakota "the land of used-to-be." When she and Manly completed the long, hot return to Mansfield, they were happy to be back in the rock house under the cool trees. They had made a trip through memories, just as Laura was traveling through memories in her writing.

Little House in the Big Woods was published in April 1932. When Laura brought the first copy to show Rose, they both were very pleased. They liked the pen-and-ink illustrations by Helen Sewell and the way Pa's stories and Laura's Wisconsin memories came to life in print.

Despite the fact that the Depression had slowed the sales of books, *Little House in the Big Woods* was a success. Children and their parents immediately loved Laura's storytelling. So did many teachers and librarians. *Little House in the Big Woods* became a Newbery Honor Book, the award given to the most outstanding children's book of the year. Laura's first royalty check for over $500 made her very happy. At sixty-five, Laura Ingalls Wilder was suddenly famous.

"I did not expect much from the book," Laura said, "but hoped that a few children might enjoy the stories I had loved." Immediately, children started writing, begging for more books. It reminded Laura of the times when Rose was little, saying, "Oh, tell me another story, Mama Bess! Please tell me another story!"

Harper & Brothers asked Laura for a second book, and she decide to write Manly's story. His boyhood in Malone, New York, was full of adventure and excitement, but getting Manly to talk about it was difficult. He said he was "not much of a hand to tell a story" and was so modest that he did not like to be the focus of attention. But Laura persisted, and collected information about Manly's ninth year on his family's farm. The book was called *Farmer Boy*, and it appeared in 1933.

Both the rock cottage and the farmhouse became places of busy writing activity. Rose's fiction now appeared in *The Saturday Evening Post*. Her pioneer story *Let the Hurricane Roar* was published there as a serial, and then became a famous book in 1933.

Laura and Rose often consulted each other about their work. When Rose started writing pioneer stories, Laura shared tales that were then used in her daughter's work. Laura relied on Rose's suggestions and advice in her own work. "Without your fine touch, it would be a flop," Laura once told Rose. Rose encouraged her, saying, "What you write is always good."

Laura still wrote in pencil, on lined school tablets that she bought at the grocery store for a nickel apiece. She wrote when she could, between fixing meals and washing dishes and other housework. Sometimes she woke from her sleep with a sentence or an idea in mind.

Quietly she moved to her desk and wrote for hours. Manly would find her asleep in the morning on the lounge, worn out with writing. When Laura completed her manuscripts, Rose typed them and sent them to New York. First they went to the agent, George Bye, and then they were delivered to Louise Raymond, her editor in the children's book department at Harper & Brothers.

When demands came for more of her books, Laura wrote *Little House on the Prairie*, which was published in 1935. It was the story of the Ingalls family's move to Indian Territory. Laura did weeks of research until she found the name of Soldat du Chêne, the Osage chief who appears in *Little House on the Prairie*. She wanted her books to be known as true stories, accurate in every historical detail. She explained that "In writing books that will be used in schools such things must be right and the manuscript is submitted to experts before publication."

Laura's memory was keen, and she found that she could improve it by "going back as far as I could and leaving it there awhile. It would go farther back and still farther, bringing out of the dimness of the past things that were beyond my ordinary remembrance."

With her first three books selling well, Laura decided to do something that had never been done before. She planned to continue writing the story of her childhood, creating a series of books. She said it would be "a historical novel for children covering every aspect of the American frontier." Laura explained that "All wanted me to go on with the story, to know what happened next."

So Laura continued to write, and Harper & Brothers continued to publish. *On the Banks of Plum Creek* was finished in 1937. Laura was seventy, and though her hair was snow white, she was energetic and active, and her blue eyes still snapped with kindly good humor.

In 1937, Laura and Manly moved one last time. They went back home. For years, they had been homesick for their old farmhouse, even though the rock house was a modern and beautiful place. Rose left the farm to do historical research at the University of Missouri in Columbia. Then she moved to New York, and finally to Danbury, Connecticut. When the Rocky Ridge farmhouse was vacant, the Wilders returned. Laura was glad to use her wood cookstove again, and to live among the surroundings Manly had built with his own hands. Once more she set up her desk in the little writing den off the bedroom and planned more books. By then, her series had a name. The stories were called the "Little House" books.

Harper & Brothers received so many requests for information about Laura Ingalls Wilder that her editor, Louise Raymond, was anxious to meet her, and to have her meet her readers. In October of 1937, it was arranged for Laura to appear at a book fair held at a department store in Detroit, Michigan. Manly had purchased a new Chrysler car, but he was eighty and decided not to drive so far himself. Instead, he asked his young friend Silas Seal to drive them to Detroit. Silas operated a gas station in Mansfield, and had once lived in Detroit. He was good-natured and patient and willing to drive the Wilders.

At the book fair Laura's appearance caused great excitement. Teachers, parents, librarians and children all crowded in to hear her speak. She answered questions and autographed books, and learned how very popular her series was.

Rose was busy in New York, working on a *Saturday Evening Post* serial called "Free Land," but she was anxious to know how her parents had enjoyed the Detroit trip. "The children all seem wildly interested and wanted to know how, where and when Laura met Almanzo and about their getting married," Laura reported in a letter. "You should have seen their faces when I spoke of it in Detroit and lots of their letters want me to hurry up and write about it."

Laura planned to finish her series with three more books, all telling about the Ingalls family's last move into Dakota Territory. Early in 1938, she worked on what became *By the Shores of Silver Lake*. She toiled for months on the book, and sent chunks of the manuscript to Rose for her comments. But in the springtime, Laura left Rocky Ridge on a trip that was both a vacation and a journey back to the land she was writing of.

Manly and Laura invited Silas Seal and his wife Neta to accompany them on a trip to the Pacific coast and back through South Dakota. The Wilders and the Seals had become close friends; Silas and Neta were so young that Manly and Laura regarded them as their children. Silas did all the driving on the 1938 trip. Laura and Neta sat in the back seat talking happily and singing songs like "Oh, Waltz Me Around, Oh Willie," and "That's Where My Money Goes."

From Mansfield, the travelers took Route 66 across Oklahoma, Texas, New Mexico and Arizona into California. They drove north along the Pacific coast to San Francisco, and then proceeded into Oregon and Washington and east to Idaho. They marveled at snow-capped mountains, mammoth redwoods, the ocean, rivers and cascades. Often Silas stopped the car so that Laura and Neta could look for wildflowers, or a picnic could be prepared.

In Yellowstone Park in Wyoming, the Wilders and the Seals watched the geyser "Old Faithful" spout. It was so early in the season that some of the roads were blocked by snowdrifts. From the road, they saw bear and buffalo and elk. After viewing all the natural wildlife and beauty of the park, the travelers continued their journey.

On the way back to Mansfield, the Wilders showed their friends South Dakota. They drove through the Black Hills to Keystone and visited Carrie. She had recently been widowed and was lonely, so Laura's visit was appreciated. Carrie was always enthusiastic about her sister's books, and eagerly added her own impressions of the family history when Laura asked.

From Keystone, the travelers drove across South Dakota to Manchester, where they visited

Grace and Nate. Laura and Manly showed the Seals their old prairie homes and the town of De Smet. Everywhere they went, the Wilders were treated with great interest because they were the parents of Rose Wilder Lane. Rose's Dakota homesteading novel *Free Land* was a well-known and best-selling book during the spring of 1938. It was very popular all over America, but especially in De Smet.

When Laura met old De Smet friends, she explained her writing project and asked for help in recalling facts and details of the town's first years. De Smet was a changed, sometimes unfamiliar place for Laura. She noted that many of the original buildings were gone. Friends had died or had moved away, but still, "Everywhere we went we recognized faces," Laura said. "But we were always surprised to find them old and gray like ourselves, instead of being young as in our memories."

So many memories of her youth in De Smet crowded Laura's writing plans that she decided on four more books to complete her series, rather than three. When she returned to Rocky Ridge after the western trip, Laura finished *By the Shores of Silver Lake*. Then she planned the rest of the "Little House" books.

17. "Our Quiet Home"

*B**y the Shores of Silver Lake* was published in 1939. It became a Newbery Honor Book, just as *Little House in the Big Woods* and *On the Banks of Plum Creek* had been. The book was eagerly awaited at bookstores, libraries and schools all over America. Laura's books were selling thousands of copies each year; no longer did she worry about income to support Rocky Ridge Farm. The royalty checks from Harper & Brothers paid more than the farm had ever earned.

Laura was grateful for her royalty checks, and she was thankful to Rose for her ideas and encouragement during the writing of the "Little House" books. In January 1939, she wrote Rose: "Yesterday, I was thinking how unbelievable it is that we are so comfortably situated. Without your help I would not have the royalties from my books in the bank to draw on."

Laura titled her next manuscript *The Hard Winter*. It described the blizzardy winter of 1880–1881 in De Smet and how the first settlers in the town survived it. In the middle of writing the book, Laura suddenly wanted to visit De Smet again.

"It was the first of June," Laura explained. "The days were lovely, warm, going-somewhere days." She and Manly decided to travel alone to the 1939 Old Settlers' Day in De Smet. Old pioneers and friends gathered annually in De Smet on June 10 for the Old Settlers' Day reunions and festivities.

"Friends thought we should not take such a trip by ourselves," Laura admitted. But Manly declared that "I have driven horses all over that country and the roads to it, and I can drive a car there." They promised Rose to drive slowly and carefully. "If we find it too hard, we can come home any time," Laura assured her.

In De Smet, the Wilders enjoyed the festivities of Old Settlers' Day. Laura collected historical information to help in her writing and made a friendly visit to Aubrey Sherwood, the publisher of *The De Smet News*. The Wilders visited three days with

Grace and Nate before driving across the plains to see Carrie in Keystone.

Laura and Manly drove with Carrie along the winding roads near Mount Rushmore, as they had done before. "We talked together," Laura said, "of childhood days and Pa and Ma and Mary."

From Carrie's home, the Wilders drove to Wyoming and Colorado, and came back home through Kansas. As always, they were glad to return home. "You folks have the prettiest place in this whole country," a friend told them, and Manly and Laura agreed.

Laura and Manly traveled no more. They settled down into peaceful days of quiet life. On Sundays, they drove to the Methodist church in town, and on Wednesdays, they went to Mansfield again for groceries and shopping. They attended church dinners and socials and liked to take long drives through the Ozark country. "I love to go for a drive as much as I ever did," Laura said.

The daily routine on Rocky Ridge still started early, with Laura cooking a seven-o'clock breakfast. Manly tended the four milk goats and the two calves in the barn. Then, he worked in the garden or in his workshop. He split wood for the range and hauled it to the house in a wagon drawn by a burro.

"We are not really farming," Laura explained. "It has been increasingly difficult to get help and lately impossible to do so at wages the farm could pay." The beautiful rock house and forty acres of land were sold. Bruce Prock and his family moved away, so the tenant house and another plot of land across the road from the farmhouse were also sold. This left the Wilders 130 acres of the land, all in pasture and meadowlands, with a timber lot for wood.

Laura's days were always busy ones. "I do all my own work," she said, "and to care for a ten-room farmhouse is no small job. Besides the cooking and the baking, there is the churning to do. I make all our own butter from cream off the goat milk. There is always sewing on hand and my mending is seldom finished."

Each day when the mailman drove by, Laura left for a half-mile walk to the mailbox. The Wilder mailbox at the side of the highway was the biggest size obtainable; every day the box was filled with mail addressed to Laura Ingalls Wilder. Classes wrote her, sending big packets of letters and drawings and photos of themselves. Teachers wrote to ask for pictures and autographs and answers to questions their students asked about the "Little House" books. Patiently, Laura answered the mail. "You would be astonished at the number of letters," Laura wrote to her new editor, Ursula Nordstrom, at Harper & Brothers. "I answer them for I cannot bear to disappoint children."

At Christmas, their loyal fans remembered Laura and Almanzo Wilder, and cards and gifts also arrived on birthdays and Valentine's Day. Laura treasured each bit of affection for her books and her family. She proudly wore an apron handmade for her by a girl in North Carolina, and carefully saved cartons of admiring mail. Because *Farmer Boy* was such a popular book in the "Little House" series, Almanzo received his share of the fan mail. "He seems to have made quite a hit with the children," Laura said in a letter to a college professor. "Almanzo was surprised and pleased that they wrote to him."

In 1940, *The Long Winter* was published. Laura's editors at Harper & Brothers asked her to change her title from *The Hard Winter*, thinking the original choice sounded too grim for a book for children. Laura cheerfully complied.

Laura worked rapidly on her seventh book, which became *Little Town on the Prairie*. In the summer of 1941, the manuscript was sent to Ursula Nordstrom. The story of Laura Ingalls' teenage years on Pa's homestead and in the town of De Smet thrilled Miss Nordstrom. "*Little Town on the Prairie*," she wrote Laura, "seems to me to be absolutely perfect. *On the Banks of Plum Creek* has up to now been my favorite but I think the new one is even better. When Nellie Oleson came into the school I almost wept with pleasure and anticipation. Every single bit of the book is perfect."

When it was published in 1941, *Little Town on the Prairie* became a Newbery Honor book, Laura's fifth. Children eagerly anticipated the next book, because in it Laura was expected to marry Almanzo. Laura also announced that the eighth book in her series would be her last. "In the next book, Laura really grows up," she said.

The last book became *These Happy Golden Years*. Stories of Laura's teaching, her courtship with Almanzo, Pa and Ma's thriving homestead and happy times in the growing town of De Smet all brought to a close the long saga of the Ingalls family.

Laura was pleased with the great interest in *These Happy Golden Years*. "It always surprises me

when one of my books is a success and I am glad
that it is selling so well," she said. Letters poured in,
praising *These Happy Golden Years*. Carrie wrote,
proud and excited with the book. Rose, too, compli-
mented *These Happy Golden Years*. "She thinks you
did a fine job on the book," Laura wrote Ursula
Nordstrom.

The final page of *These Happy Golden Years* included the line "The End of the Little House
Books." Laura was seventy-six and ready to retire
from eleven years of steady writing. "It seems that
my mind is tired," she explained. "It refuses to work
again on a book." George Bye, the New York agent
who managed all of Laura's business with her publisher, encouraged her to continue writing. He offered her the chance to write magazine stories and
assured her that Harper & Brothers wanted more
books. But Laura explained that she wanted to
"spend the rest of my life living it, and not writing
about it."

And so Manly and Laura settled into golden
years at the end of their lives together. When their
work in the house and garden was through, they
played cribbage and read their magazines and papers. They enjoyed drives and dinners with Neta

and Silas Seal. Neta always cooked special meals for the Wilders' February birthdays.

Both Manly and Laura remained keenly interested in politics and world events. Their newspapers and the radio kept them informed of the news of World War II. Since the Wilders grew so much of their own food, they were not much affected by the wartime food rationing. Their trips in the Chrysler were limited by gas rationing, though; no longer could they think of a summer trip to South Dakota. As Laura explained to a distant friend she could no longer visit, "Our rubber is good, but our gas is short." Laura mourned along with the rest of America when she heard of fearful wartime battles and loss of life. "In our quiet home," Laura said, "it is hard to believe such terrible things are happening in the world."

Despite the difficulty of travel, Carrie was able to travel to Mansfield by train from Rapid City, South Dakota, in the fall of 1944. It was an exciting reunion. "The love of our early childhood," Laura told her, "has followed you all the way." Carrie enjoyed visiting with Laura's friends and making short drives through the Ozark Mountains. Grace had died in 1941, and Laura had to write children that

"Sister Carrie and I are the only ones of our family now living."

Laura, Carrie and Rose decided together that Pa's fiddle should be preserved in a museum. South Dakota seemed to be the right place for such an important part of the Ingalls history. Laura's books were appreciated there and were often promoted by Aubrey Sherwood in *The De Smet News*. A student from Watertown, South Dakota, wrote Laura, "I think you have helped a lot of boys and girls become interested in their own state. After my teacher finished *The Long Winter*, one of the kids said 'I never knew South Dakota had a history like that!'"

So Pa's fiddle went back to the prairie. It was accepted by the South Dakota State Historical Society and kept on display for many years in the museum across from the capitol building in Pierre. Children and adults constantly stopped at the museum to see the fiddle. The greatest pleasure Laura received from her writing was the knowledge that Pa would not be forgotten. In this she knew she had succeeded.

So many children begged Laura for another book that she was half-persuaded to begin one. "I find myself constructing sentences and situations in what might be another book," Laura admitted. "I must begin to think about it," she decided. Finally, Laura told Ursula Nordstrom that "I will see if I can make the new book jell."

Daily living finally crowded out the time Laura sought for writing another book. Manly was close to ninety, and he and Laura both complained how hard it was to hire any help for the house, yard and garden. Rose was permanently settled in Danbury, Connecticut, too far away to do anything but advise her parents through her letters. "We like to live here, but wish our only child did not live so far away," Laura said.

The Wilders had one last great adventure equal to any they experienced in their early days on the prairie. On April 12, 1945, the same day that President Roosevelt died, a terrific cyclone blew through the Ozarks. Rocky Ridge farmhouse stood solid, though one of the big living-room windows was blown out and shingles from the roof were scattered. The yard suffered more damage. Big, old oaks were uprooted, split and twisted, and trees were thrown across the driveway.

For two weeks the Wilders could not drive out of the yard and there was no telephone or electricity. The Seals made their way out to Rocky Ridge, but many days passed before the trees could be cleared away. "It was quite a return to former times being isolated with our coal oil lamps for lights," Laura reported. "You see Almanzo and I have had still another adventure and escaped."

Laura wrote Carrie to assure her that she and Manly were safe after the Missouri cyclone. It was one of Laura's last letters to her sister. In June of 1946, Carrie died. She was buried with the rest of the Ingalls family in the cemetery in De Smet.

While the Wilders were living life on Rocky Ridge, Laura's books were becoming internationally famous. Immediately after World War II, the United States State Department, at the urging of General Douglas MacArthur, arranged for "Little House" books to be translated into German and Japanese. Because Laura's books provided an accurate picture of American life, he believed that Germans and Japanese would benefit from reading them.

Letters immediately started coming to Laura from Germany and Japan. Translations of the "Little House" books were published in several other countries as well, much to Laura's amazement.

"Though you are far away and speak a different language," Laura wrote to the Japanese children, "still the things worth while in life are the same for us all and the same as when I was a child so long ago."

In America, Laura's fame constantly grew. Librarians and teachers and families still stopped to see the Wilders and were shown around the house and yard by Manly and Laura. Children in the Pacific Northwest voted Laura their favorite author, and she was presented with the Harry Hartman Award. In 1947, a poll of 55,000 Chicago children clearly showed Laura was their favorite writer. This led to a celebration of Laura's eightieth birthday in Chicago.

A department store there held a birthday party in Laura's honor on February 7, 1947. Laura and Manly were invited to attend and to appear on "The Hobby Horse" radio program, but they could not go. Manly was ninety and not strong; Laura would not leave him. So that the children would not be too disappointed, Laura mailed 200 autographs to the store, and a letter telling all about her life since the "Little House" books. She closed her letter with this message to her young readers:

The Little House books are stories of long ago.

The way we live and your schools are much different now, so many changes have made living and learning easier. But the real things haven't changed. It is still best to be honest and truthful; to make the most of what we have; to be happy with simple pleasures and to be cheerful and have courage when things go wrong.

The "Little House" books sold so well that Harper & Brothers arranged to publish new editions, with new illustrations. Garth Williams was selected to do the new drawings. Since he knew little of the country described in the books, he decided to travel west to see it for himself.

The first stop on Garth Williams' trek into the past was Mansfield. In September 1947, he arrived to see the Wilders. As he drove through the gate at Rocky Ridge, he spied Laura, picking up walnuts. When they went into the house to talk with Manly, Garth was almost overwhelmed. "Imagine!" he marveled. "Here I stood with the hero and heroine of the 'Little House' books. What could be more exciting!"

Garth Williams went on to visit all the places Laura wrote about. When his travels were over, he began to re-create the "Little House" life in his illustrations. It would take him six years to finish his work.

The Wilders knew they were important in bookstores, libraries and schools across America. Even so, they never forgot their long tradition on Rocky Ridge. They were eager to keep the land dedicated to farming, and they were concerned over what might happen to their beloved home in the future. They knew that Rose was not interested in returning to the Ozarks.

A young couple, Harland and Gireda Shorter, had purchased the rock house and part of Rocky Ridge in the early 1940's. The Wilders watched their farming operation with interest, and in 1948 they made a decision. They wanted the Shorters to have the farm.

One Sunday morning, Laura telephoned the Shorters and asked them to come for a visit. When they arrived, she and Manly sat on the porch swing and offered to sell the Shorters their house and all of the remaining Rocky Ridge Farm. They could pay fifty dollars a month and allow the Wilders to live there for the rest of their lives. The agreement was made; Manly said he was glad to have the steady monthly income.

Surprising news came to the Wilders in December 1948. The Detroit Public Library planned to open a new branch library and name it for Laura Ingalls Wilder. It would be the first library in the city named for a living person and for a woman.

Laura was amazed at the news. Unfortunately, she had to say she could not attend the dedication planned for the spring of 1949; Manly was too feeble to be left alone. But Laura helped with the preparations by sending a message to be read at the ceremony, along with the original manuscripts for *The Long Winter* and *These Happy Golden Years*, which were to be presented to the library.

Manly planted the garden during the spring of 1949, but at ninety-two he moved slowly and sometimes painfully. In July, he suffered a serious heart attack. Laura nursed him faithfully through his recovery. Neta and Silas Seal helped; they brought groceries and food and drove Laura to town when she needed to go. Neta often slept on the porch during the nights, in case Laura needed help.

Through the early fall, Manly improved. But on Sunday morning, October 23, he had a second heart attack. Laura quickly called Neta and Silas to come. But by the time they arrived, Manly had died.

18. A Rich Harvest

Friends drew close to Laura when Manly died, and Rose arrived from Danbury for his funeral. Mansfield had lost one of its oldest pioneers, and Manly was missed. Readers all over America mourned along with Laura when the news of Almanzo Wilder's death spread.

Laura bravely bore the loss of her husband of sixty-four years. "It is quiet and lonely here now," she wrote a friend. She was weary after the long weeks of nursing Manly, and she was uncertain about what to do next.

Friends urged Laura to move into town, or to invite someone to live with her at Rocky Ridge. Laura said that she was not timid about living alone, and her loneliness for Manly would be the same in Mansfield or with someone in the house. She decided to stay on at Rocky Ridge.

Laura was surrounded by kind friends and neighbors during her years alone. Neta and Silas visited her often and invited her to their house. The Elmores, who lived in Bruce Prock's old house across the road, dropped in to visit. And the Jones family, who lived close by, became Laura's faithful companions. The two Jones boys, Roscoe and Sheldon, stopped to see Laura nearly every day on their way home from school. They brought her mail, helped with chores around the house and became her special friends.

It pleased Laura to know that the "Little House" books were read at bedtime to Roscoe and Sheldon. But the boys could listen to those stories from Laura herself. Often they gathered around Laura with their cousins, the Shorter boys, and listened to her tell of her days in the woods and on the prairies.

In the spring following Manly's death, another library honored Laura. On May 12, 1950, Pomona, California, dedicated the children's department of its library as the Laura Ingalls Wilder Room. Laura's gift to the newly established room was the original penciled manuscript of *Little Town on the Prairie*. An annual celebration of Laura's February 7 birthdate was started in Pomona; it featured gingerbread made from Laura's recipe and a fiddler to play the songs Pa had played.

Laura's birthdays always brought stacks of greetings to her. In February 1951, more than a thousand cards and gifts arrived at Rocky Ridge. For weeks she was busy reading and responding to the overflow of affection for her. Among the birthday wishes was a cablegram of congratulations from General Douglas MacArthur.

Later in 1951, Mansfield made plans to honor Laura by naming the local library for her. She had worked hard to establish the county library in Mansfield, and her books were an important part of the library's collection, so the honor was well deserved. On September 28, 1951, the dedication of the Laura Ingalls Wilder Library was held.

Laura was so modest that people doubted she would attend the library dedication. Although she had received many honors, they always embarrassed her. But because she did not want to disappoint her friends who had arranged the tribute, for the first time Laura was present at a ceremony in her honor. When she entered the high school auditorium, the Mansfield schoolchildren sang her a song of greeting and the band played.

Standing behind huge baskets of flowers on the stage, Laura told the group of children, librarians, teachers and townspeople how proud she was of the library and the friendship of her hometown. "I can only say I thank you all!" she exclaimed. "From my heart, I thank you!"

People at the library dedication always remembered how beautiful Laura looked that day, and how jolly and friendly she was. The Springfield newspaper sent a reporter to write about the event. In an article titled "Mansfield Honors Great Lady," Laura was described as "a striking, charming little woman."

"Her white hair was piled high," the paper said, "and held in place by a gold comb that matched her large earrings. She wore a beautiful, very dark red velvet dress, at the shoulder of which a friend had pinned a large orchid. It was difficult to believe that she was 84 years old."

A Laura Ingalls Wilder display case was established in the new library, and Laura helped to fill it. She presented the library with autographed copies of her books, pictures and gifts sent to her from foreign countries, and mementoes of her girlhood. On her Wednesday visits to town, Laura stopped at the library for her week's reading. She especially enjoyed mystery stories and westerns, and the librarians always saved the new ones for her.

Springfield, the closest big city to Mansfield, had its own chance to honor the author of the "Little House" books. In the fall of 1952, during Children's Book Week, Laura traveled to Springfield with a friend for an autograph party at a bookstore. She sat on a small stage at the back of the store and was amazed to see readers stretching out into the street. Laura graciously signed books, talked and accepted little presents brought by boys and girls.

In the line, waiting to visit with Laura, was Carrie Preston, the Springfield children's librarian. Mrs. Preston had loved Laura and her stories for many years and encouraged scores of children to read the "Little House" books. She brought a "Little House" book with her to show Laura. It was a library copy, read so many times that it was ragged and worn. On the last page, a child had written, "I love you, Laura." Carrie Preston thought, as she spied Laura happily chatting with the children: "We all do."

Although the loneliness for Manly remained keen, Laura was warmed by the affection of her wide family of readers. Daily, the table next to her rocking chair in the dining room was heaped with mail. During the summers, a regular stream of out-of-state travelers stopped to see her. Old friends came, some from De Smet, but most of Laura's visitors were strangers to her. They came from Indiana, California, New York, Pennsylvania—indeed, from across the country—all hoping to meet the author of the "Little House" books.

Laura joked that she thought summer vacationers must outdo farmers at rising early; one family came knocking at her door to meet her at seven o'clock in the morning. Good-naturedly, Laura entertained her callers. Many of the visitors were children, and Laura said she could never refuse to meet a child.

Local children came to visit, too. Some rode their bicycles out to Rocky Ridge, or walked over the hills to the Wilder farmhouse. Laura invited them to sit with her in the porch swing or served milk and cookies at the kitchen table. Sometimes she played the old pump organ in the parlor or took them to explore the big farmhouse with her. But best of all was when Laura told stories. She sat in her rocking chair, and the children gathered around her on the cool green dining-room floor.

While Laura loved telling children about the past, she was intensely interested in the present. She read every word of the weekly *Mansfield Mirror*, and when her friends from town came to visit, she always asked, "What's new in Mansfield?" She listened to her radio for news of the world and read many magazines. She studied politics and economics. Each Wednesday while she was in town, Laura stopped in at the *Mansfield Mirror* office to discuss current events with the editor.

Once when a friend who was Laura's age confided that she was ready to die, Laura quickly replied that she wanted to see what would happen next in the world. "The only way to go is ahead," she said. Besides, she wanted to live beyond the age of ninety, because Manly had.

In the fall of 1953, the "Little House" books received great fanfare when the newly illustrated editions by Garth Williams were published. Everyone at Harper & Brothers awaited Laura's reaction to the carefully researched drawings. When she saw the first of the reillustrated "Little House" books, Laura was delighted. She immediately sent a telegram to her publisher saying: "Mary, Laura and their folks live again in these illustrations."

The new editions sold quickly and renewed interest in Laura's writing. *The Long Winter* was dramatized for a radio broadcast, and there was talk of a television series based on the books. What pleased Laura most was the knowledge that more and more boys and girls were reading the "Little House" books. "When writing down those memories of my long ago childhood," she said, "I had no idea that they would be so well received. It is a continual joy to me that they are so well-loved."

In 1954, Laura celebrated her eighty-seventh birthday with two parties in Mansfield and the usual overflow of mail from her fans. "There is some advantage in being my age," Laura told her agent, George Bye. "Everyone is glad I am 87 years old!"

News of yet another honor came to Laura around the time of her birthday. The American Library Association sent her a telegram, announcing the creation of a Laura Ingalls Wilder Award. The award, a medal, was to pay tribute to authors who had written lasting and important books for children. Laura was the first recipient of the gold medal, which was designed by Garth Williams. But Laura could not attend the award ceremonies in

Minneapolis. "Being 87 years old with a tired heart I have to avoid excitement even if pleasant," she explained.

As she grew closer to ninety, Laura said she was "quite well usually, but must be slow and careful to keep that way." She still tended her mail, went to church and to town and cooked and cleaned on Rocky Ridge. But she admitted, "There are days when I lie down most of the time to let my tired, old heart rest."

Rose visited from Danbury and that always cheered Laura. Rose flew from New York City to Springfield, where Laura and the Mansfield taxi driver met her with Laura's Oldsmobile for the drive home. Rose usually spent several months on Rocky Ridge with Laura each year. Together, they called on friends, did needlework and marveled at the success of the "Little House" books. Rose was still very busy as a writer, and Laura liked hearing her clattering typewriter again, upstairs on the sleeping porch.

When Laura was eighty-seven, she had her first airplane ride! After one of Rose's visits in Mansfield, Laura returned to Danbury with her by plane. From covered wagons to airplanes, Laura was still ready for adventure. She enjoyed seeing Rose's beautiful house and gardens, but she did not stay in Danbury long.

Laura was most comfortable at home on Rocky Ridge. There were memories there and familiar things. She needed to be home, she said, to feed her cat and the turtles who appeared at the kitchen door for bread and milk. "They come up out of the hollow to see how I'm doing," Laura explained.

Laura stayed alone at Rocky Ridge until Thanksgiving 1956. Rose arrived to visit and immediately she knew that Laura was not well. Laura became so ill that Rose took her to the hospital in Springfield. The doctors discovered that Laura had diabetes.

For many weeks, Laura rested in the hospital. Rose stayed nearby. News of Laura's illness spread, and the children of Springfield signed a twelve-foot scroll with their names, urging her to "get well soon." One boy wrote that he would rather read her books than watch television. The scroll was delivered to Laura's hospital room, and it cheered her.

"She looks and feels better than she has for years," Rose told friends in December. But Laura was eager to go home. When she was well enough, on the day after Christmas, Laura returned to Rocky Ridge with Rose.

Laura's ninetieth birthday approached. In libraries and classrooms and little houses all over the world, people remembered. Children colored and cut and pasted, making special greetings for Laura. With their teachers' help, they addressed their cards to Rocky Ridge Farm in Mansfield, Missouri.

Laura did live to be ninety, just as Manly had. Three days after her birthday, on February 10, 1957, she died. There was great sadness in Mansfield and in Missouri and throughout the world, when newspapers and radio reported the news of Laura's death.

"My love will be with you always," Laura assured Rose in her last message to her child. Rose knew that many had shared her mother's love. She also knew that Laura's storytelling would only increase that love. "The longest lives are short," Rose said. "Our work lasts longer."

For Laura Ingalls Wilder, pioneer, wife, farmer, mother and author, the work she had done would last. The "Little House" books were her richest harvest.

Index